IRELAND
and
BRITISH
POLITICS
from
1870-1921

Audrey M Hodge

Russell Rees

COLOURPOINT PRESS

The Colourpoint Logo
The Colourpoint is one of the most beautiful of all the long-haired cat breeds. Persian in temperament and shape, it has the coloured points of the Siamese on the face, ears, paws and tail. The Colourpoint logo depicts a real blue-cream point kitten, Lady Jane Grey, and was drawn by Rhoda McClure, a fifth form art student at Omagh Academy, Co. Tyrone.

© Audrey M. Hodge
 Russell Rees
 1993

First published by
Colourpoint Press, 1993.
Reprinted 1994.

ISBN 1 898392 00 5

Layout and design: Norman Johnston
Cover design: MainStreet, Hillsborough,Co.Down
Typeset by: Colourpoint Press
Film output by: Typeform Repro, Dublin
Printed by: ColourBooks, Dublin

Colourpoint History texts are only available by direct order from the publishers:

COLOURPOINT PRESS
Omagh Business Complex
Gortrush
Omagh
Co. Tyrone
BT78 5LS

The Authors

Audrey M. Hodge M.A. and Dr. Russell Rees are both practising history teachers with many years' experience of the Northern Ireland curriculum. They were co-authors of the best-selling "*Ireland, Britain and Europe from the late 16th century to the early 18th century*", published by the Western Education and Library Board in 1992.

Audrey Hodge obtained her M.A. in Modern and Contemporary History at the University of Ulster. She is the author of "*Gallows and Turnkeys*", a short history of Omagh Gaol.

Dr. Rees graduated in History with honours at the University of Ulster and his doctoral thesis dealt with the Northern Ireland problem between 1945 and 1951.

Acknowledgements

The authors and publisher would like to thank the following for permission to reproduce the illustrations listed below:

Linenhall Library, Belfast: 9E; 11D; 13E; 18A; 20A; 22A,B; 26A; 27D; 28A; 29F; 30A; 31G; 33F; 34A; 36A,B; 37D; 40A,B,C; 41D,E,F,G; 43E; 44A,C; 45D; 46A; 47D; 48A,C; 49F; 50H; 51J,K,L; 54A,C; 56A; 58A; 60B; 61E; 62A; 64A; 72B.

Public Record Office of Northern Ireland, Belfast: 11E; 14A; 38A; 39E; 42B; 47F; 48A; 59E; 68A; 72C.

The Trustees of the Ulster Museum, Belfast: 25F; 69C; 70A.

National Museum of Ireland, Dublin: 6A; 52A; 63C; 65D; 66A.

National Library of Ireland, Dublin: 16A; 23F; 63D.

Milligan collection: 20B.

McFarland collection: 42A; 43C.

The illustrations on the front and rear covers are from the collection of the Linenhall Library, Belfast.

Contents

Introduction

Ireland began the 19th century with a new system of government. Under the terms of the **Act of Union (1800)**, the Irish Parliament disappeared, and as the title of the act suggests, Great Britain and Ireland were joined in the United Kingdom. Throughout the 19th century, Members of Parliament (MPs) from all parts of Ireland sat in parliament in London. Although Roman Catholics could vote, no Roman Catholic was allowed to be an M.P. until **1829** when the **Catholic Emancipation Act** was passed.

DANIEL O'CONNELL

This Emancipation Act had been a victory for Daniel O'Connell, a Catholic lawyer, who had founded a movement called the **Catholic Association**. After winning Catholic Emancipation, O'Connell turned his attention to the Union. In 1840 he formed the **Repeal Association** which campaigned for the repeal (removal) of The Act of Union and the return of a separate Irish Parliament. Like the earlier Catholic Association, the Repeal Association enjoyed the support of Catholics of all social classes. Such movements, which tried to use public opinion to achieve their aims like the repeal of the Union, were unusual anywhere in Europe in the first half of the 19th Century, because as the poorer groups in society could not vote in elections they generally displayed little interest in politics.

One other special feature of O'Connell's campaigns for emancipation and repeal was the involvement of the Catholic Church. Parish Priests performed the vital task of local organisation, acted as a link between O'Connell and the people and helped to supervise the huge crowds which attended the political meetings all over the country. Despite the powerful campaign for repeal of the Union, the British Government stood firm and the movement eventually fizzled out with O'Connell's death in 1847.

FAMINE

Perhaps an important reason for the failure of the Repeal movement was the impact of the potato famine which devastated Ireland in the late 1840's. Before the famine the population of Ireland had grown rapidly with many families living on tiny plots of land and almost totally dependent on the potato crop for their existence. As a result of the famine about one million people died from starvation and disease and another million fled from the hunger on board overcrowded emigrant ships bound for Britain and the USA. Many Irish people blamed the government for failing to implement effective famine relief measures, and this encouraged a feeling of hatred against Britain which was particularly strong among the Irish emigrant population in the USA. Later, Irish-Americans were to lend enthusiastic support to various schemes designed to end British rule in Ireland. Despite the failure of Irish farms to provide enough food for the population during the famine years, Ireland remained a predominantly agricultural country for the rest of the century and beyond, and it was only really in North East Ulster that any significant industrial development took place.

YOUNG IRELAND

The Repeal Association led by O'Connell was a very moderate peaceful movement, but within the movement a small section of younger, more extreme followers formed a new group which became known as **Young Ireland**. The Young Ireland group later broke away from O'Connell. The Young Irelanders wanted to make Irish people see themselves as different from the English. To spread their ideas they had founded a weekly newspaper called **The Nation**. This was an appropriate title, because the Young Ireland leaders wanted the people to think of Ireland as a separate nation. The newspaper contained many articles which emphasised the differences in language, history and culture between Ireland and England. However, the Young Irelanders also believed that if the British government rejected repeal, they should fight to obtain their freedom from Britain. When it later became clear that repeal was impossible, the Young Irelanders staged a rebellion in 1848. The result was disastrous. The rebellion had been very badly planned and with most of the people still suffering from the effects of the famine, there was little support for the Young Irelanders. In such circumstances it was no surprise that the 1848 rebellion was a dismal failure.

FENIANS

Another rebellion, which tried to win independence for Ireland by using force, occurred in 1867. This was known as the Fenian Rising. The Fenians were a group which had been formed in 1858 with the aim of overthrowing British rule and establishing an independent Ireland. Although the Fenian Rising enjoyed more support, including help from the USA, than the Young Ireland rebellion, it too ended in failure.

This form of violent nationalism was obviously very different from O'Connell's moderate approach. As we have already noted, O'Connell received great help from the Catholic clergy during the repeal campaign, but it was the members of this same clergy who were very much opposed to the Fenian movement. To be a Fenian involved taking an oath and joining a secret society, and the Catholic church was against secret oath-bound societies which it regarded as sinful and a threat to its own position.

Although violent nationalism failed totally in its objective of ending British rule in Ireland, it was still a significant force. The Fenian Rising of 1867 kept alive the violent nationalist tradition and provided an example for future generations which would be prepared to take up arms to win independence for Ireland.

**IRELAND BEFORE 1921,
SHOWING THE PLACES
MENTIONED IN THE TEXT.**

© WNJ

1.1 The Growth of Nationalism

SOURCE **A**

A Gaelic League poster contrasting an independent Ireland with Ireland governed from London.

Nationalism is a very powerful emotion which can often lead to great rivalry between different nations. Most historians see the growth of nationalism as something that occurred in Europe during the 19th century. Then much of Europe was controlled by powerful states which ruled over various nationalities in their empires. One such empire was the Austrian Empire. It contained eleven nationalities, and during the course of the 19th century it came under increasing pressure from some of these different national groups, which wanted to gain independence from Austria so that they could form their own independent country or **nation-state**.

Nationalism emerged as a powerful force in 19th century Europe for a number of reasons. For most of the leaders of the different national groups nationalism meant progress and prosperity. They thought that it would lead to a more peaceful Europe with increased co-operation between the new nation-states. Finally, they also thought that nationalism would create a fairer system of government, thereby ending rule by foreigners who cared little for the various national groups under their control.

Nationalism contains a number of key elements. The most obvious of these is **geography**. A clearly identifiable piece of territory which is cut off by national boundaries forms the basis for

SOURCE **B**

"Those who speak the same language are linked...they understand each other and are capable of communicating more and more closely with one another..."

Johann Fichte (1762-1814)
- a German philosopher.

any nation-state. The natural boundaries could be rivers or mountains, or, in the case of an island, the sea would form a natural frontier. A second element is **race**. Nations usually contain people who are from the same race or ethnic group. This means they will share many common characteristics, the most obvious being the colour of their skin. Perhaps the easiest way to recognise someone from a particular country is by listening to the **language** they speak. People who share a common language are easily identified as being distinct, and the language can be used to unite such people making them feel part of a separate nation. A fourth element is **culture**, and any distinct national group will share the same cultural background. Each country, therefore, might have its own literature, music, customs, national games and folklore. One final element which can sometimes be used to define a particular nation is a common **religion**.

The last element presented a particular problem for Ireland. The country was mainly Catholic, but throughout Ireland there were a substantial number of Protestants. The situation was further complicated by the fact that many of these Protestants were concentrated in North East Ulster, and here they even formed a sizeable majority. The language was another difficulty for Irish nationalism. For most of the 19th century the Gaelic language was in decline, as most families had come to see English as a more useful language in their everyday lives. Indeed, one side effect of the famine was to reduce substantially the number of Gaelic speakers, because many of its victims came from the poorer south and west, where Gaelic was widely spoken. By 1851 only about a quarter of the population spoke Gaelic, and this was to fall steadily over the next forty years.

When a movement to revive the Irish language began in the 1890s, it was described as **cultural nationalism**. Irish people were encouraged to play Irish games, sing Irish songs, play Irish music, read Irish literature and, of course, speak the Irish language. All this made them feel distinct or separate from Britain. This was a different form of nationalism from the type we saw Daniel O'Connell proclaiming. Indeed O'Connell was not interested in cultural nationalism. Instead he sought to make changes by getting a majority of MPs in parliament to support reforms which would bring improvements to Ireland. To increase his influence he had organised support among ordinary Irish people. We can describe this as **constitutional nationalism**. It had moderate aims which were to be achieved only by peaceful methods. As we have seen, this moderate peaceful form of nationalism was rejected by groups like the Fenians. They believed that Ireland should have complete independence from Britain, and in order to gain this freedom the Fenians believed they were justified in using force to overthrow British rule. We can describe this as **violent nationalism** or **revolutionary nationalism**. All three forms of nationalism were to become significant in Ireland during the late 19th and early 20th centuries.

SOURCE C

"In ...Europe we have more than twice as many nations as states and that means that...states must be composed of more than one nation."

Thomas Masaryk (who was later President of Czechoslovakia), speaking in October 1915.

SOURCE D

"This royal throne of kings...this blessed plot, this earth, this realm, this England."

Spoken by John of Gaunt, in William Shakespeare's play *Richard II*.

SOURCE E

"Nationalism consists of all those people who have been persuaded that they share in the national grievance."

From *Nationalism* by Kenneth Minogue.

1   Which sources use the following as factors of Nationalism:
    (a) language
    (b) opposition to other groups
    (c) pride in one's own country?

2   How useful are these sources in helping you define the term "Nationalism"?

1.2   The Origins of Home Rule

After the failure of the Fenian Rising in 1867 many Irishmen began to look at the alternatives to violent nationalism. One of these was **Isaac Butt**, a Protestant lawyer from Co Donegal. Butt had earlier been in close contact with the Fenians, because he had defended some of the movement's leaders who had been brought to trial after the rising. Although he admired the honesty and dedication of all these men, he soon became convinced that an armed rebellion or insurrection could never succeed. Butt believed that what was needed was a much more moderate solution which would not threaten Britain's interests in Ireland and could be achieved by peaceful or constitutional methods. With this in mind he formed the **Home Government Association** in 1870. Within a few years the movement changed its name to the **Home Rule League**, and in 1874 the Home Rule party contested the general election winning 59 seats. Constitutional nationalism was once again the dominant theme in Irish politics.

The central aim of the Home Rule movement was to obtain a parliament in Dublin, which would be in charge of Irish affairs. Significantly, the Home Rulers were demanding control over only internal affairs, such as education and road building, thus leaving other important external matters, such as trading links and peace treaties, under the control of the parliament in London. This was a more moderate objective than Repeal, but the Home Rule party saw this as an advantage, because the English parliament at Westminster might be persuaded to grant such a small concession. After all, although Home Rule would mean the creation of a separate Irish parliament, its powers would be strictly limited, leaving the English government in overall control.

Of the 59 Home Rule MPs who had been returned at the 1874 general election only about 20 of them could be considered as enthusiastic politicians who were dedicated to the Home Rule cause. This meant that, at the beginning, the Home Rule party did not work as an effective, united group of MPs in the House of Commons. Another drawback for the new party was that it lacked decisive leadership. Butt was much too gentlemanly to fight hard for Ireland's cause in parliament. He did not want to annoy other MPs and he was too often absent to provide the dynamic leadership that the movement required.

However, a number of other Home Rule MPs were prepared to adopt a more hostile approach. Chief among these was **Joseph Biggar**, a Belfast butcher, who had been elected MP for Cavan in 1874. Biggar's idea was that he and some of his colleagues would make a nuisance of themselves in the House of Commons by delaying parliamentary business. They did this by speaking for hours in parliamentary debates and making the House of Commons sit all night. In this way they obstructed the progress of every bill through parliament. This new strategy was known as **parliamentary obstruction**, and while such action proved very unpopular among other MPs, it was nevertheless

SOURCE A

" ...We claim the privilege of managing our own affairs by a parliament assembled in Ireland"

" ...There should be in Ireland an administration for Irish affairs, controlled by the Irish parliament"

From *Proceedings of the Home Rule Conference held in the Rotunda, Dublin, 18-21 November 1873.*

SOURCE B

" No man has the right to fix the boundary to the march of a nation. No man has the right to say to his country 'Thus far shalt thou go and no farther', and we have never attempted to fix the ne plus ultra [limit] to the progress of Ireland's nationhood and we never shall."

From a speech by C.S. Parnell in Cork, 22 January 1885.

SOURCE C

"As for the men whom misgovernment has driven into revolt, [i.e. the Fenians] I say for them that if they cannot aid you, they will not thwart your experiment."

From a speech by Isaac Butt.

SOURCE D

"[The Home Government Association] was a curious alliance at first, embracing a number of Protestant supporters motivated by actual resentment of Gladstone's new measures, particularly a feeling of betrayal over the disestablishment of the Protestant Church."

From *The Bold Fenian Men* by Robert Kee, 1972.

SOURCE E

Cartoon from *Punch* 6 March 1880

THE AWKWARD HORSE
(OF THE PARLIAMENTARY BUS.)

Northcote: "Steady Hartington! I don't want to put the 'twitch' on but if we must we must."

successful in arousing even more interest in the Home Rule cause back in Ireland. In fact, Biggar's obstruction policy was so effective that Parliament later had to make radical changes to its procedures in order to prevent further attempts to disrupt the business of the House of Commons in this way.

During the period of parliamentary obstruction a new figure appeared in Irish political life. His name was **Charles Stewart Parnell**, and he had been elected in the Co. Meath by-election of 1875. In his first speech as an MP in the House of Commons, Parnell revealed his nationalist opinions: 'Ireland is not a geographical fragment. She is a nation'. It was, therefore, clear from the outset that Parnell would present a more determined challenge to the English government than the moderate approach followed by Butt. Parnell was very different from the rest of his colleagues in the Home Rule party. He was a Protestant landowner who had been educated in England. Tall and distinguished looking in appearance, he spoke with a distinctly English accent and behaved like an English country gentleman. Yet in many ways these differences were ideal for a leader, because they made him stand out from his followers. Soon, Parnell was to challenge Butt's leadership. By 1877 he already had more influence than the aging Butt, and with the latter's death in 1879 Parnell became the undisputed leader of the Home Rule party. The movement was now ready for a new departure.

?

1 How do the aims of Home Rule in Source **A** differ from those in Source **B**?

2 How does Butt think the members of the Fenian movement will react to the new Home Rule Movement? (**C**)

3 According to Source **D** why did Protestants support the Home Rule cause at first?

4 How does Source **E** help to illustrate the obstructionist policy of the Home Rulers in Parliament?

5 Why was the Home Rule movement attractive to so many groups when it was formed? (**A**, **B**, **C**, **D** and **T**)

1.3 The Land Question

Parnell realised that if the Home Rule cause was going to enjoy widespread support in Ireland, then the parliamentary party would have to be linked more closely to the ordinary citizens. This meant that some sort of alliance would have to be formed with the tenant farming class. In the late 1870s, however, the tenant farmers were facing very severe problems with the result that they had little time for any interest in politics. Their difficulties were caused by a combination of very bad weather and a dramatic fall in agricultural prices in 1878-79. For the poorest farmers, many of whom lived in the west of Ireland, paying the rent for their land became impossible, and this led to many tenant farmers and their families being evicted. It was this crisis in the countryside which caused farmers to unite against the threat of eviction. The man who organised their resistance was **Michael Davitt**.

Davitt had been involved in the Fenian movement, and in 1870 he received a lengthy prison sentence in England when he was found guilty of acting as an arms agent for the Fenians on the mainland. Released in 1878, following an appeal by Parnell, Davitt returned to Ireland after a brief visit to the USA where he met the Irish-American Fenian leader, **John Devoy**. On his return Davitt, a native of County Mayo, was determined to organise combined action by the tenant farming class to protect their livelihoods.

THE LAND LEAGUE

In order to make his organisation effective throughout the country Davitt knew he would have to win Parnell's support. Consequently in June 1879, the Home Rule leader was invited to address a protest meeting of tenant farmers in Westport, Co Mayo. By now it was clear to Parnell that most Irishmen were much more interested in the land question than in Home Rule, and in Westport he was given a great ovation when he urged his audience to resist eviction and hold on to their homesteads. Later in 1879, the **Land League** was formed to organise and co-ordinate opposition to evictions.

This new body had two aims. In the short term it wanted to stop evictions and reduce the rents paid to the landlords, while in the longer term it wanted to ensure that the tenants would replace the landlords as owners of the land. Parnell became President of the Land League on its formation, and this helped to seal the alliance between Home Rule and the land question. The linking of the political objective of a Home Rule parliament in Dublin to the social and economic goal of land reform, leading eventually to tenants becoming outright owners of their farms, was known as the **New Departure**. This new departure was given an additional boost by the support of Irish-Americans whose financial assistance enabled the League to carry on the struggle with the landlords.

SOURCE A

"Now what must we do in order to induce the landlords to see the position? You must show them that you intend to hold a firm grip of your homesteads and lands ... You must help yourselves, and the public opinion of the world will stand by you and support you in your struggle to defend your homesteads."

From a speech by C S Parnell at Westport, Co. Mayo, 8 June 1879.

SOURCE B

"The Land League's object was, by promoting the organisation of the tenant farmers, to bring about a reduction in rents, protect those threatened with eviction, and finally obtain 'such reform in the laws relating to the land as will enable every tenant to become the owner of his holding by paying a fair rent for a limited number of years'."

From *The Bold Fenian Men* by Robert Kee, 1972.

SOURCE C

"... Captain Boycott, the manager of Lord Erne's estates in Co. Mayo. Local people refused to work for him in Lord Erne's house or on his land. Labourers were brought in from Ulster, protected by hundreds of police and troops, but life became so unbearable for Boycott that he had to leave. From then on the word 'boycott' was used for this sort of action. In this case Lord Erne reduced all rents by a tenth so the boycott was successful."

From *Modern Ireland* by E G Power, 1988

SOURCE D
Cartoon in *Punch*, 5 Feb 1881.

STRANGLING THE MONSTER.

SOURCE E
Cartoon (1886), depicting Gladstone, and titled *The Cause of Order*.

THE LAND WAR

Opposition to the landlords was simple and effective. They used the American money to erect temporary accommodation for evicted tenants, but as the number of evictions increased, a new tactic was adopted. If a family was evicted, the League tried to prevent the landlord or his agent from re-letting their land. This was achieved by **boycotting** any other tenant who agreed to rent the farm in question. He would be shunned by the community and treated as an outcast. If this failed, violence, or the threat of violence, would be likely to follow. The increase in evictions after 1879 and the Land League's response led to widespread upheaval in the three years from 1879-82. This became known as the **Land War**.

Alarmed by the power of the Land League, the English government felt it had to make concessions in an effort to reduce tension in the Irish countryside. Consequently, a **Land Act** was passed in **1881** which went some way to addressing the grievances of tenant farmers. The act established Land Courts in an attempt to ensure that fair rents were charged, and it also prevented the eviction of any tenant who had paid his rent.

Still, for Davitt and Parnell the 1881 Land Act did not go far enough. Too many of the poorest farmers living on very small plots of land were not protected by the act and nothing was done for those who were behind on their payments.

Agitation in the countryside would continue.

?

1 What was the significance of involving Parnell in the land question? (**A** and **T**)

2 What were the aims of the Land League? (**B** and **T**)

3 Is it true to say that "boycotting" was the most successful method used by the Land League? Explain your answer. (**C** and **T**)

4 Study Sources **D** and **E**.
   (a) How do they portray the Land League and its members?
   (b) What impressions of Gladstone are given in these cartoons?
   (c) Account for the differences in the two cartoons.

5 Construct a timeline showing six important stages in the history of the land question. (**T**)

1.4 Irish Nationalists and British Liberals

THE KILMAINHAM TREATY

With the Land League continuing to challenge the authorities, the government was convinced that firm action was necessary. By the end of 1881 Parnell was imprisoned in Kilmainham Jail, Dublin, but this led to increased violence as evicted tenants began to use force against the landlords. This violence was on such a scale that the government realised the situation was now beyond its control, and it would have to make a deal with the League to end the Land War. The government's response was an offer to help tenants who had fallen behind with their rents. In return, Parnell, who was released after six months in Kilmainham Jail, promised to use his influence to restore peace in the countryside. This deal between Parnell and the government was called the **Kilmainham Treaty**.

After his release in May 1882 Parnell realised that the way forward was to concentrate on the political objective of Home Rule. He himself had been alarmed by the scale of violence and intimidation shown during the final year of the Land War, but Parnell was able to use this chaos in the countryside to increase support for Home Rule. It was easy to argue that if Ireland had its own parliament in Dublin dealing with internal affairs, the kind of injustice experienced by the tenant farmers could be prevented. From 1882, therefore, the demand for Home Rule had clearly become more important than the campaign for further land reform.

PARNELL AT WESTMINSTER

The general election of 1880 had been a great personal triumph for Parnell. Under his leadership the Home Rule MPs, or Irish Nationalists as they were called at Westminster, began to work together as a co-ordinated group. This was vital, because Parnell knew that Home Rule could only be obtained through the efforts of a strong, united and disciplined body in parliament. Yet as far as numbers in the Westminster parliament were concerned, the Irish Home Rule Party formed only a small minority. Politics at Westminster were dominated by the two main parties, the **Liberals** and the **Conservatives**. It was clear to Parnell that if Home Rule was to be passed in parliament, it would require the support of one of the two great parties.

PARNELL AND GLADSTONE

Fortunately for Parnell and the Irish Nationalists, the leader of the Liberal party was **William Ewart Gladstone**, a politician of great ability who had long been sympathetic to Irish grievances. Gladstone had been Prime Minister from 1868-74, and following the general election of 1880 he returned as leader of the new Liberal government. During his first term as Prime Minister he had shown that he wanted better treatment for Ireland by introducing a number of reforms in parliament. Indeed in one of his most famous statements he said, 'My mission is to pacify Ireland'. This was why he was very concerned about the

SOURCE A

" The Province of Ulster was evenly divided ... between eighteen nationalist Home Rulers (who were mainly Catholic and represented constituencies principally in the west and south of the Province) and seventeen anti-Home Rule Conservatives (who were Protestants and largely represented constituencies in the eastern and more prosperous part of the Province)."

From *Home Rule and the Irish Question*, by Grenfell Morton, 1980.

SOURCE B

'Before this wrong all the other wrongs of Ireland do grow pale, For they've clapped the pride of Erin's isle into cold Kilmainham jail.'

From a contemporary ballad.

SOURCE C

'In a private letter on the day he was imprisoned Parnell admitted that the Land League movement was already breaking up fast. The principal cause of this was the success of the new Land Act.'

From *The Bold Fenian Men*, by Robert Kee, 1972.

SOURCE D

'The Chief Secretary for Ireland, W E Forster, had felt betrayed by Gladstone's decision to release Parnell, and had resigned.'

From Robert Kee, *ibid*.

SOURCE E

From *Punch*
30 Jan 1886

THE LIVE SHELL

(Which of 'em will throw it overboard?)

<-- *Gladstone*   *Lord Salisbury* -->

widespread violence in the Land War and introduced the 1881 Land Act in an attempt to remove the fears expressed by tenant farmers and to reduce tension in the countryside. While the 1881 act had been only a limited success, Gladstone was becoming increasingly impressed by Parnell and his arguments in favour of Home Rule.

PARNELL AND THE CATHOLIC CHURCH

For his part Parnell was happy to see a return to normality after the Land War. Not only did the restoration of order allow him to focus attention on the Home Rule issue, but it also led to the Catholic Church in Ireland throwing its weight behind the Home Rule movement now that it was firmly back on the constitutional or peaceful track. This suited Parnell, because he intended to use the support of the Catholic clergy to help him win votes when the next general election took place. His opportunity arrived in 1885.

THE 1885 ELECTION

The 1885 general election marked a major breakthrough for the Home Rule party. It won a total of 86 seats, 85 in Ireland and one in Liverpool where there was a large Irish immigrant population. Overall the results showed that the Liberals had won a total of 333 seats which easily made them the largest party in the House of Commons. Their great rivals, the Conservatives, had won only 251 seats. Yet there was great disappointment for the Liberals because they had only just failed to secure the overall majority which Gladstone desperately wanted. He knew that if the Conservatives and the Home Rule party combined, they could defeat any measure which his government might propose. Therefore, although the Irish party had only 86 seats, Parnell now held the balance of power and consequently was in a very strong position.

?

1   How many (a) Conservative and (b) Irish Party MPs were elected for Ireland outside Ulster? (**A** and **F**)

2   Source **A** was written almost one hundred years after the election of 1885. Does this mean it is unreliable as evidence? Give reasons for your answer.

3   Source **B** is a ballad written at the time of Parnell's imprisonment. How valuable is this type of source to anyone studying this period?

4   What does Source **C** tell us about Parnell's feelings on the future of the Land League?

5   (a) What can we learn from Source **D** about the attitude of other Liberals to Gladstone's actions over Ireland?

   (b) How adequate is this source in helping you make a comment about Liberal attitudes in general?

6   Source **E** is a cartoon. Is such a source reliable as evidence? Explain your answer.

SOURCE F

General Election figures 1885			
	Liberals	Conservatives	Irish Party
England and Wales	271	223	1
Scotland	62	10	0
Ireland	0	18	85
Totals	333	251	86

1.5 The First Home Rule Bill 1886

The 1885 election results had created uncertainty at Westminster. Disappointed by the fact that he had not obtained enough seats to form a majority government, Gladstone resigned, and **Lord Salisbury** agreed to lead a new Conservative government. However, as the Conservatives had only won 251 seats, it was unlikely that they would be able to remain in power for long. In fact, Salisbury resigned at the end of January 1886, after his government was defeated in the House of Commons when most of the Irish party voted against him. By February 1886, therefore, Gladstone was back as Prime Minister.

GLADSTONE'S CONVERSION TO HOME RULE

The election results had tied the Irish Nationalists and British Liberals together. Parnell knew that co-operation with the Liberals would bring most advantages to the Irish, while Gladstone appreciated that the Irish party, now a united force under Parnell's expert leadership, could no longer have its wishes ignored at Westminster. Earlier, in December 1885, Gladstone's son, Herbert, stunned the political world by informing the Press that his father had been converted to the principle of Home Rule. Undoubtedly, the general election results had been a major factor in bringing about this transformation in Gladstone's thinking, but declaring his support for Home Rule represented a huge gamble, because many influential Liberals remained bitterly opposed to any suggestion of Home Rule.

THE BILL IS INTRODUCED

Nevertheless, Gladstone took the risk of splitting the Liberal party, and on 8 April 1886 he introduced a **Home Rule Bill**. His speech to the House of Commons on this occasion was a remarkable feat. Gladstone, now seventy-five years of age, delivered a three-and-a-half hour speech in which he described how Westminster's previous efforts to control Ireland by **coercion** (force) had failed, and he appealed for the House to support this new course of action. The Liberal leader concluded by stressing: 'We stand face to face with Irish nationality'. In these circumstances he believed that the only way forward was to give the Irish control over their internal affairs. Conservative MPs were outraged.

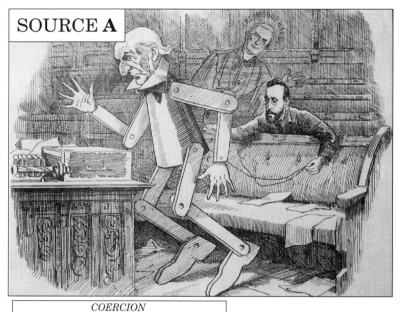

SOURCE A

COERCION
He can talk by the yard, he can plot and can plan,
And Home Rule hymns can sing;
But where is the good of this Grand Old Man
If it's Healy that pulls the string?

From:
The Coming? Gladstone
Tim Healy was MP for Cork and one of Parnell's closest supporters.

SOURCE B

"We stand face to face with what is termed 'Irish Nationality'...The Irishman is profoundly Irish, but it does not follow that because his local patriotism is keen, he is incapable of Imperial patriotism."

From a speech by Gladstone in the House of Commons on the First Home Rule Bill, 1886.

SOURCE C

"We look upon the provisions of this bill as a final settlement of this question and I believe that the Irish people have accepted it as such a settlement."

From a speech by Parnell in the House of Commons on the First Home Rule Bill, 1886.

PARNELL AND THE BILL

During the parliamentary debate which followed, Parnell welcomed the bill even though he must have been disappointed by some of its clauses. For example, on taxation, the bill did not recognise that Ireland was considerably poorer than England in terms of her resources and productivity, and it was proposed that Ireland should make a large financial contribution to Westminster every year. Still, every Home Rule MP who spoke in the debate supported the bill despite the strict limitations which were to be imposed on the proposed new parliament in Dublin. Certainly, the measure came nowhere near the total separation of Britain and Ireland, which the Young Irelanders and Fenians had fought for a few decades earlier.

THE BILL DEFEATED

When it came to a vote on the bill, Gladstone knew he could count on the support of the 86 Home Rule MPs. The crucial question, therefore, was how many Liberal MPs would join with the Conservatives in opposing the measure. In the end 93 Liberals voted against the government, and the first Home Rule Bill was defeated by 343 to 313.

Those Liberals who opposed Home Rule did so for two reasons. Firstly, they believed that there could be no halfway-house between the union of Great Britain and Ireland and the complete separation of the two countries. Secondly, they shared with the Conservatives a fear of the impact which such a concession might have on the British Empire. In particular, concern was expressed about India, because many thought that if Ireland was granted Home Rule, there would follow an immediate demand for Indian self-government. Ultimately, it was feared that this could result in the disintegration of the Empire.

THE 1886 ELECTION

Gladstone rejected these arguments. For him, granting Home Rule to Ireland was not only the correct action to take politically, it was also the right thing to do morally. He was convinced that public opinion in Britain would support him, and following the bill's defeat in the House of Commons he resigned in June 1886 and called another general election. When the election results were announced, however, it was clear that the majority of English voters were against granting Home Rule to Ireland. The Conservatives had won 316 seats making them the largest party in the House. Lord Salisbury formed a new government, and a new Irish policy was devised. Despite this setback, Gladstone remained committed to the principle of Home Rule.

SOURCE D

'But the right honourable member for West Birmingham [Mr. Joseph Chamberlain] has claimed for Ulster a separate Legislature for that Province of Ulster. Well Sir, you would not protect the loyal minority of Ireland, even supposing that you gave a separate Legislature to the Protestants of Ulster, because there are outside the Province of Ulster over 400,000 Protestants who would still be without any protection...'

From a speech by Parnell in the House of Commons on the First Home Rule Bill, 7 June 1886.

1 What evidence is there in Source **A** to support the view that Gladstone was the "puppet" of the Irish Nationalists?

2 How is Gladstone attempting to lessen the fears of those Liberals who opposed Home Rule, on the grounds that it would help lead to the disintegration of the Empire? (**B** and **T**)

3 What are the strengths and weaknesses of using only Parnell's version of the effects of the Home Rule Bill? (**C** and **D**)

4 What reasons are given in this section to explain why the 1886 Home Rule Bill was defeated?

1.6 The Parnellite Split

Following the defeat of the 1886 bill, Parnell spent most of his time in England trying to win popular support for the Home Rule cause. It was clear that support for constitutional nationalism in Ireland had reached its peak and that the future success of the measure would depend on the fortunes of the Liberal party in Britain. Back in Ireland, however, the defeat of the Home Rule Bill once again focused attention on the land question.

Two of Parnell's most able associates, **William O'Brien** and **John Dillon**, were determined to help poor farmers who were suffering from the effects of a new agricultural depression which was at its worst in the 1886-88 period. The usual pattern of rural crisis in Ireland was being repeated. Tenant farmers were receiving lower prices for their produce, and with their incomes reduced they had great difficulty in meeting their rent payments. Consequently, evictions were on the increase. O'Brien and Dillon responded by launching a **Plan of Campaign**, which saw united action by tenants in each local area to decide on the level of rents which they would insist the landlords charged. Parnell was opposed to this new agitation in the countryside because he believed it brought bad publicity to the political campaign for Home Rule in England, where he, of course, was engaged in trying to attract new supporters.

BALFOUR

To meet this challenge, Salisbury appointed a new Chief Secretary for Ireland early in 1887. This was his nephew, **Arthur James Balfour**, a very gifted politician who would later become Prime Minister. Balfour's aim was to persuade the Irish to drop their demand for Home Rule. To do this he decided to adopt a 'carrot and stick' policy. On the one hand he would ensure that severe punishment was handed out to those guilty of breaking the law, while on the other he was determined to show the Irish that the English government would give fair treatment to those tenants who were in economic difficulties. Accordingly, a new **Land Act** was passed in **1887**, which reviewed existing rent charges and linked the level of all newly fixed rents to agricultural prices. This meant that when prices for agricultural produce fell in poor years, rents would be reduced. By this Balfour laid the foundations for a new Conservative policy which was followed over the next twenty years. The Conservatives believed that by granting a series of concessions to Irish farmers they would voluntarily give up their demand for Home Rule. This policy was known as **Killing Home Rule with Kindness**.

THE PIGOTT FORGERIES

It was during 1887 that Parnell's interest was aroused by a very strange episode. A number of letters appeared in **The Times** linking Parnell to several violent outrages committed by extreme nationalists in Ireland. Immediately, alarm spread through Westminster, and a government enquiry was set up to investigate the allegations. When it was later established that all

SOURCE A

MRS. PARNELL IN 1880

Kitty O'Shea

SOURCE B

"As usual, the Land War had a two way significance as regards Irish Nationalism. On the one hand it showed how the everyday issue of the land, a social issue, took precedence in Irishmen's minds over the political national issue...On the other hand the bitterness of each phase of the Land War consolidated emotional feeling against the government and indirectly strengthened general 'National' feelings."

From *The Bold Fenian Men*
by Robert Kee, 1972.

SOURCE C

"But the fact remains that the 'English wolves' and the Irish bishops express the same opinion about him and he cannot mend the matter by calling nicknames..."

From the North Kilkenny by-election manifesto. (Quoted in *The Times*, 11 December 1890.)

the letters had been forged by **Richard Pigott**, an Irish journalist who had run into financial difficulties, Parnell's name was cleared and his popularity rose both in England and Ireland. Parnell was now at the height of his power and his position as the leader of Irish nationalism seemed secure. Yet disaster was not very far away.

THE O' SHEA DIVORCE

In February 1890 Captain William O' Shea, a former Home Rule MP, brought a divorce case against his wife, **Katherine O'Shea**, and named Parnell as the guilty third party. The Irish leader had first met Katherine in 1880 and they soon became lovers. The two lived together in England and had three children, the first of whom died in infancy in 1882. Many of Parnell's political colleagues knew about his affair with Mrs O' Shea and ignored the association, but when details of their relationship hit the headlines in the divorce court proceedings, Parnell found himself under attack from several quarters. For a start, Gladstone wrote to the Home Rule party informing them that he would drop his support for Home Rule if Parnell continued to be their leader.

Meanwhile in Ireland it became increasingly clear that most Home Rule supporters had been shocked by the revelations about Parnell's affair with Mrs O' Shea. One very influential body which had been particularly perturbed by the affair was the Catholic Church. Of course, Catholic teaching was very opposed to any form of divorce. Although Parnell was a Protestant, the vast majority of the Home Rule MPs and their supporters were Catholic, and naturally the church sought to use its influence to have Parnell removed from the leadership of the party. Surprisingly, Parnell himself believed that he would emerge from the divorce crisis with his position intact. However, while he retained the loyalty of a number of Home Rule MPs, the majority were turning against him. Those opposed to Parnell, who were called the **anti-Parnellites**, realised that Home Rule would only succeed if the alliance with the Liberal party was retained, but this would be broken unless Parnell resigned as leader. Eventually, the question of Parnell's leadership would have to be decided by a vote among the Home Rule MPs.

THE FALL OF PARNELL

The final act in this leadership crisis was played out in Committee Room 15 in the House of Commons. Many bitter words were exchanged before the MPs voted. The result was a devastating blow to Parnell. 32 MPs pledged their support, but there were 54 opposed to him. The party which Parnell had, almost single-handedly, moulded into an effective political force was now torn apart.

SOURCE D

"It was not that withstanding the splendid services rendered by Parnell to his country, his continuance at the present moment in the leadership would be productive of consequences disastrous in the highest degree to the cause of Ireland...[and] would render my retention of the leadership of the Liberal Party almost a nullity."

Letter from Gladstone to John Morley, 24 November 1890.

?

1 In what ways was the land question in late 19th century Ireland linked to the Home Rule issue? (**B** and **T**)

2 Explain how the O'Shea divorce scandal ruined Parnell's political career? (**C**, **D** and **T**)

3 What effect do you think Gladstone's reaction to the divorce scandal had on
(a) Parnell and
(b) his fellow Liberals?
Explain your answer. (**D** and **T**)

4 How had the attitude of British Conservatives towards Home Rule changed in the period 1880 to 1887? (**T**)

1.7 The Second Home Rule Bill 1893

SOURCE A

"A PRIVATE VIEW"

PAT. 'What d'ye think of the Home-Rule Bill, Murphy?'

MURPHY (puzzled). 'Begorra, if it means staying at home with the ould woman every blessed day, Home-Rule won't do for me at all!'

PUNCH 22 April 1893

Despite this rejection by his fellow MPs, Parnell was not prepared to give up his position without a fight. He returned to Ireland and toured the country during the winter of 1890-91, making speech after speech in a valiant effort to rally support. Although his speeches aroused considerable sympathy among the public, Parnell came to realise that there were powerful forces operating against him. Indeed, the influence of the Catholic bishops, who now openly voiced their disapproval of Parnell, was revealed during three by-elections which were fought in 1891. The three seats contested were **North Kilkenny**, **North Sligo** and **Carlow,** and in each case Parnell's candidate was soundly beaten by an anti-Parnellite.

In these by-elections, Parnell's support came from the more extreme nationalists who had sympathised with the Fenians, and in some of his speeches he certainly appeared to be appealing directly to the Fenian tradition. In fact, after his death extreme nationalists used some of Parnell's 1891 speeches to win support for their objective of securing independence for Ireland by force of arms.

THE DEATH OF PARNELL

The by-election defeats had been another bitter blow for Parnell, but he still refused to consider the prospect of even temporary retirement. By the autumn of 1891, however, he was ill following his exertions in Ireland. Although he carried on the struggle to the end, he died in England in **October 1891** leaving Irish nationalism without its most able leader. Parnell's funeral, which was held in Dublin, was the largest to take place in the city since O'Connell's in 1847.

THE SECOND HOME RULE BILL

A **general election** in **1892** brought Gladstone back to power as leader of a new Liberal government. Again, the Liberals required the support of the Irish Nationalists to give them an overall majority. In Ireland 80 Home Rulers had been elected, and it was clear that Irish voters supported the continuation of the alliance with the Liberal party, because the anti-Parnellites had won 71 seats, while the Parnellite section of the party had won only 9 seats. Still, all the Home Rule MPs expected Gladstone to introduce a new Home Rule Bill. The Liberal Prime Minister did not disappoint them, and in February **1893** Gladstone, now aged 84, introduced the **Second Home Rule Bill**. The new bill was very similar to the plans outlined in the 1886 measure. The only real changes were a reduction in the number of Irish MPs at Westminster and the exclusion of the Irish MPs from voting on measures which affected only England, Scotland and Wales

To many people's surprise, the second Home Rule Bill was passed in the House of Commons by a majority of 34. The Irish Nationalists were jubilant, but this jubilation was short-lived. For a bill to become law it also had to be passed in the House of Lords and here the Conservatives enjoyed an overwhelming majority. Everyone knew that the Lords would reject the bill, which they did in September 1893 by 419 votes to 41.

GLADSTONE'S RETIREMENT

Although Gladstone was keen to call another election, the Liberals had learned from the mistakes of 1886 and the Cabinet refused to have another election on the issue of Home Rule. Soon afterwards, Gladstone retired from politics. He had been a towering figure in British politics for over 50 years and had made strenuous efforts to come to terms with Irish nationalism. Now Home Rule was viewed as a practical solution to the Irish problem and many Irish Nationalists were convinced that the establishment of a Home Rule parliament in Dublin was inevitable.

However, it was also clear that with Gladstone's retirement nothing would be achieved in the immediate future. In addition, both the Irish Nationalists and the English Liberals realised that before Home Rule could become law, something would have to be done about the House of Lords, where the Conservatives would continue to block any Home Rule measure. For the moment, therefore, constitutional nationalism seemed to have gone as far as it could.

SOURCE B

'But when it appears to me that it is impossible to obtain Home Rule for Ireland by constitutional means, I have said that ...'I will in a moment so declare it to the people of Ireland and, returning at the head of my party, I will take counsel with you as to the next step.' '

From Parnell's speech during the Kilkenny by-election, 1890.

SOURCE C

'The 1893 Home Rule Bill eventually occupied more parliamentary time than any other bill in the history of the century...Four hundred and thirty-nine speeches were made for it in the Commons and nine hundred and thirty eight against.'

From *The Bold Fenian Men* by Robert Kee, 1972.

?

1 Source **A** is a cartoon. How do you think this affects its reliability?

2 In what ways would Source **B** be useful to an historian studying Parnell's place in Irish Nationalism?

3 What can we learn from Source **C** about the impact of the Second Home Rule Bill on the House of Commons?

1.8 The Gaelic Revival

While constitutional nationalists remained optimistic about the prospects for Home Rule, they also recognised that its success would depend on the existence of favourable circumstances at Westminster. The Home Rule Party's policy was to wait on the sidelines until these circumstances came about. For the ordinary people, however, whose minds had been stirred by nationalist publicity, there would be no waiting on the sidelines. Indeed, a significant number had become unhappy about the Irish Party's failure to obtain Home Rule, and they were seeking other ways to express their nationalism. One thing was clear; they were **Irish** not **English** and they wanted to show this. Therefore, before the end of the 19th century a new movement, which helped to encourage the growth of national awareness, was underway. It was known as the **Irish Ireland Movement** or **Gaelic Revival**.

SPORT AND LITERATURE

The Gaelic Revival led to a cultural re-awakening. There was an upsurge of interest in Irish games, Irish music, Irish literature and the Irish language, all of which were expertly publicised. Back in 1884 the **Gaelic Athletic Association (GAA)** had been formed in Thurles, Co Tipperary, by **Michael Cusack**. Its aim was to promote the Irish games of Gaelic football and hurling to replace foreign or English games such as cricket, rugby and tennis, and it proved an immediate success.. By 1889 the GAA had a membership of 50,000 and it was particularly strong in rural areas.

On the literary front the key figure was **William Butler Yeats**, a Protestant poet from Co. Sligo. Yeats provided the inspiration for a new wave of writers, poets and playwrights, most of whom came from the West of Ireland and worked around the turn of the century. All of them wrote of Ireland's past focusing on the lifestyle of the ordinary Irish peasant. In this way they were able to increase awareness of Ireland's rich cultural heritage and develop a keener sense of national identity.

SOURCE A

Arthur Griffith

SOURCE B

At the Giant's Causeway, Co. Antrim, about 1895.
Left to right: Seaton Milligan, Douglas Hyde, Miss Hyde (his sister).

THE GAELIC LEAGUE

Probably the most important new movement formed in this period was the **Gaelic League**. It was founded in **1893** by **Douglas Hyde**, the son of a Protestant minister from Co. Roscommon, and **Eoin MacNeill**, a young Catholic civil servant who had grown up in Glenarm, Co. Antrim. Its aim was to stimulate the revival of the Irish language which by then was spoken only in small communities in remote parts of the west of Ireland. Hyde, in particular, was anxious that the language movement would stay out of politics and he hoped that the League would attract Irishmen of different religious and political beliefs. After a slow start, the League's influence spread throughout Ireland. Whereas the GAA was strong in rural areas, the Gaelic League had its success in the towns, where large numbers of educated, young, mainly middle-class men and women joined the movement. Despite Hyde's wishes, it was almost inevitable that the League would become a political force, attracting more advanced nationalists who were unhappy with the Home Rule Party. It was from among this group that the leaders of a more extreme form of nationalism would later emerge.

One other figure who must be mentioned in any discussion of the Gaelic Revival was **D P Moran**. A very gifted writer and journalist, Moran expressed his opinions in the columns of his own weekly newspaper, **The Leader**, which he founded in **1900**. While he supported the work of the Gaelic League, he saw the revival of the Irish language merely as a step in the creation of a separate Gaelic civilisation and a distinct Irish nation which, in time, would probably seek complete independence from Britain. Moran's work gave the Irish Ireland movement publicity and helped to generate a wider political debate on Ireland's future.

SINN FEIN AND THE IRB

A key figure involved in this debate was **Arthur Griffith**. He rejected the policy of Home Rule which he believed did not go far enough to meet the hopes of most Irishmen. In the columns of the weekly newspaper, **United Irishman**, which he edited, Griffith campaigned for greater independence for Ireland and urged Irish people to buy Irish-made products rather than British goods. Griffith was also very critical of the Home Rule MPs, and proposed that Irish representatives should refuse to attend Westminster and establish their own parliament and government in Dublin. In **1905** Griffith founded a new political movement, **Sinn Fein**, to win support for his ideas. Where Griffith differed from other advanced nationalists, however, was in his opposition to the use of violence to achieve any political objective. At the same time, another group, which had no such qualms about using force, had been stirred by the Irish Ireland movement. This was the old Fenian movement or **Irish Republican Brotherhood (IRB)** as it had become known. The IRB saw how it could infiltrate and use movements like Sinn Fein and the Gaelic League to further its aim of overthrowing British Rule in Ireland.

Although the Gaelic Revival captured the attention of many Irish people at the turn of the century, groups like Sinn Fein and the IRB remained small, though significant, movements on the fringe of Irish politics.

SOURCE C

'It has been hinted to us that it is our opinion that no one but a Catholic can be an Irishman. We never said so, nor do we think so... When we look out on Ireland we see that those who believe...in Ireland a nation are, as a matter of fact, Catholics... As we are for Ireland, we are in the existing circumstances on the side of Catholic development... If a non-Catholic nationalist Irishman does not wish to live in a Catholic atmosphere let him turn Orangeman.'

From *The Leader*, 27 July 1901.

SOURCE D

'The Gaelic League and the Leader aim at stimulating the old peasant Papist aboriginal population, and we care very little about the others, though I would not let this be seen as Moran has done.'

Douglas Hyde to Lady Gregory, 7 January 1901.

?

1 Yeats and Hyde were Protestants from southern Ireland, and MacNeill was a Roman Catholic from Co. Antrim. How do these facts support or deny the views expressed in Sources **C** and **D**?

2 Write a letter to a newspaper in 1901, expressing the views of a supporter of the Gaelic Revival and giving your reasons why such a revival has an essential role to play in the Irish Nationalist movement.

2.1 The "Black North"

The Irish problem was complicated by the existence of another group of people in the country who did not share the enthusiasm of the constitutional nationalists for Home Rule. These people were fiercely opposed to any moves to grant even such a limited measure of freedom as Home Rule. At all costs they wanted to maintain the Union with Britain, and this is why they were called **Unionists**. Only a minority in Ireland, they possessed enormous wealth and power, much of it derived from their ownership of the land. These Unionists were **Protestants**, and while they were split into various Protestant denominations, they were united in the defence of their position within the Union. Although they were scattered throughout Ireland, they were particularly strong in North-East Ulster where they formed a majority of the population.

THE ORANGE ORDER

Most Ulster Protestants were the descendants of the English and Scottish settlers who had arrived in the province during the **Ulster Plantation** in the 17th century. With them they brought their Protestant religion. Not surprisingly, there was tension between the new settlers and the native Irish, and this occasionally resulted in outbreaks of violence. In **1795** Ulster Protestants came together to form the Orange Society or **Orange Order** which they used to protect their interests. Interestingly, the trouble that resulted in the formation of the Orange Order had not been caused by a religious quarrel, but by a succession of land disputes.

Towards the end of the 18th century the population of Ulster, like the rest of Ireland, was booming. It was growing particularly rapidly in Co. Armagh, and here land-hungry Catholics were infuriating local Protestants by offering higher and higher rents for farms which the Protestants had previously occupied. It was this economic competition for land in Co. Armagh which caused a violent Protestant reaction and the formation of the Orange Order. While its membership declined during prolonged periods of peace, the Orange Order would later become a vital movement for the political organisation of the Protestant community in Ulster.

THE LINEN INDUSTRY

The province of Ulster had escaped the worst ravages of the Great Famine which had devastated large areas of the south and west of Ireland. Farmers in the North were usually slightly better off than their counterparts in the rest of the country, because they did not depend exclusively on farming for all of their income. They earned this extra money by weaving **linen** in their own homes and then selling the cloth to merchants who travelled the countryside. This was known as cottage industry and it was common all over Ulster.

SOURCE A

Postcard c1912

SOURCE B

BELFAST UNDER HOME RULE. Making a site for the statue of King John I of Ireland   A propaganda postcard.

2.1

By the middle of the 19th century, however, linen production had moved out of the home and into the factory. This change was part of the **Industrial Revolution** which had swept through much of Britain in the late 18th and early 19th centuries. Yet as far as Ireland was concerned, the Industrial Revolution had been confined not just to Ulster, but to a small area in North-East Ulster. This was the region around Belfast and the Lagan Valley. By the second half of the 19th century this area was clearly very different from any other part of Ireland. Large mills with tall chimney stacks dominated the landscape, while the noise of giant steam-driven engines filled the air.

The impact of the Industrial Revolution certainly brought increased prosperity to Ulster, but it also had the effect of strengthening economic and trading links with mainland Britain. For the leading industrialists and many of their workers the link with Britain was considered vital to their continued economic prosperity. It was no surprise, therefore, that these people were prepared to go to any lengths in order to maintain the Union.

SOURCE C

"Shipbuilding was male, mostly Protestant, and a symbol of the Union or 'Britishness'. Linen was much more mixed."

From *Belfast - Portraits of a City* by Robert Johnstone, 1990.

SOURCE D

"Linen and ships made Belfast utterly different from any other place in Ireland, and perhaps helped alter the political fate of the whole island."

From Robert Johnstone, *ibid*.

SOURCE E

"Environment had conditioned Ulster Protestants from the first to be self-protective and self-reliant in a potentially hostile situation. What motivated them was always their self-interest."

From *The Bold Fenian Men* by Robert Kee, 1972.

SOURCE F

A Belfast linen mill

?

1 How did the North of Ireland differ from the rest of the country? (**D**, **E** and **T**)

2 Study Sources **A** and **B**. Which political group(s) were most likely to produce these? Give reasons for your answer.

3 Read all the sources and the text and explain why people in the North wished to keep the Union.

2.2 — Belfast - A Divided Industrial City

Belfast was by far the most important industrial city in Ireland. As a manufacturing centre it ranked alongside the new industrial cities in the North of England. Indeed, to contemporary travellers Belfast in the second half of the 19th century was much more like Liverpool, Manchester or Glasgow than Dublin or any other Irish city. With its slums and bad sanitation, Belfast shared all the social problems of the other Victorian industrial cities which had been created by the Industrial Revolution.

SECTARIAN DIVISIONS

In 1800 its population was estimated at just under 20,000, but during the 19th century Belfast became the fastest growing city in the British Isles. By 1850 its population was over 100,000, and by 1900 this figure had climbed to nearly 400,000. The textile industry was booming and large numbers were attracted to the city seeking employment in the linen mills. Many of these newcomers were from the south and west of Ulster, especially from the densely populated county of Armagh, and they brought their religious rivalry with them. Tension between the two communities was never far from the surface and consequently as the city grew rapidly, Catholic and Protestant working class districts of the city became clearly identified. This **segregation** was, of course, determined by a desire for protection against possible attack from the other community. In fact, religious or **sectarian** rioting was becoming a familiar feature as the city developed from the mid-century onwards. These riots, which were usually confined to the summer months, were particularly bad in 1857, 1864 and 1872. Therefore, segregation and serious sectarian divisions were entrenched before the political problems of Home Rule appeared in 1886.

SHIPBUILDING

Perhaps even more impressive than textile manufacturing was Belfast's shipbuilding industry which grew from the 1850s onwards. This industry was dominated by the firm of **Harland and Wolff**. These two men, Edward Harland and Gustav Wolff, were at the forefront of the new technology for the production of modern iron and steel ships, and their expertise and reputation attracted a growing list of orders for naval and passenger ships. Another shipyard opened in 1879. This was **Workman and Clark**, which specialised in smaller ships, but it closed down when economic recession struck in the early 1930s. Harland and Wolff employed only 500 men in 1861, but by 1900 this figure had risen to 9,000. Meanwhile, the numbers employed in the linen industry, where men, women and children laboured together for long hours in hot, dusty, often dangerous conditions, rose from 55,000 in 1871 to 69,000 by 1896.

ENGINEERING

Shipbuilding was important, because while it did not provide as many jobs as linen manufacturing, it required skilled workers who received considerably higher wages. The construction of new ships provided a further boost to Belfast's engineering industry, which had earlier developed to meet the growing demand for linen machinery. Now these engineering firms began to manufacture steam engines, water

SOURCE A

"One of the most astonishing social phenomena in the history of the Union was the growth ... of the city of Belfast... Belfast's population of 20,000 at the time of the Union had expanded more than ten times that number by the late 1880's... The population of Dublin in the same period only doubled. At the same time Belfast ... became one of the most thriving industrial cities of the United Kingdom... Belfast became an outpost of industrial Britain."

From *The Bold Fenian Men* by Robert Kee, 1972.

SOURCE B

"In Belfast they had large steel and iron ship-building yards where fathers and sons could be employed. They also had what was termed their staple industry, the linen industry, where the wives and daughters found employment. If there was not sufficient employment in these places they had the largest rope manufacturing establishment in the world."

Speech by James Henderson, Lord Mayor of Belfast, to the Irish Trade Union Congress in 1898.

SOURCE C

"In 1864 there were 225 Roman Catholics working for Harland and Wolff, who were criticised for failing to act decisively against sectarianism ... by 1887 only 77 Roman Catholics were left."

From *Shipbuilders to the World (Harland and Wolff)* by M.Moss and J. R. Hume.

turbines and other components necessary for the production of ships. Another related industry which became very important in the second half of the 19th century was Belfast's ropeworks. It produced the very thick, strong rope used by ships when they tied up in port.

Belfast, therefore, was a very imposing industrial city unlike any other in Ireland. By the end of the 19th century it had the largest shipyard in the world, the largest linen mill, the largest ropeworks and the largest tobacco factory. The Belfast area was one of the world's most important industrial centres. Yet despite this prosperity, the city also had its particular problems. Large numbers of poor working class families occupied slum dwellings in different parts of a city divided along religious lines. This was to provide the background for the very serious sectarian violence which lay ahead.

SOURCE D

"In 1886 Harland, as Mayor, was one of the main organisers of the campaign against [Home Rule]. Harland and Wolff threatened to move to the Clyde if Home Rule was granted, though secret plans had already been made to move to the Mersey."

From M. Moss and J.R. Hume, *ibid*.

SOURCE E

"Religious problems in the workforce [Harland and Wolff] recurred ... In 1872 during the tension surrounding the Home Rule debates, which led to rioting in the town, 500 men left work early and fought a battle with police ... Catholics were being forced out of their homes in Protestant areas ... from which the Harland and Wolff workforce was largely drawn."

From M. Moss and J.R. Hume, *ibid*.

SOURCE F

The launching of the *Titanic* at Harland and Wolff's shipyard in Belfast in May 1911. Eleven months later, on 15 April 1912, *Titanic* sank on her maiden voyage with the loss of 1503 lives.

?

1   What were the four main industries in Belfast? (**T**)

2   What would have attracted people to Belfast in the 19th century? (**A**, **B** and **T**)

3   What evidence of sectarianism is there in Belfast at this time? (**C**, **E** and **T**)

4   How can we tell from Source **D** that the owners of Harland and Wolff were unhappy about Home Rule?

5   Write a short letter from a Roman Catholic shipyard worker, who has lost his job, to a friend explaining what has been happening in Belfast.

2.3 Links with Britain

SOURCE **A**   A contemporary postcard

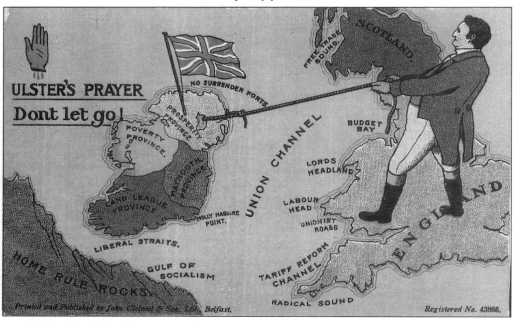

In addition to its industrial importance, Belfast also became a thriving port. It was here that coal, the vital raw material of the Industrial Revolution, was brought from the British coalfields. Of course, this coal also provided the fuel for the new age of rail transport. The first railway in Ulster ran from **Belfast to Lisburn** and opened in **1839**. If Ulster's industry depended on Britain for the supply of raw materials, it was equally dependent on mainland markets for its exported manufactured goods. Linen cloth was sold to Britain and to many parts of the British Empire. The ships produced by Harland and Wolff were sent to the Royal Navy or to the great British shipping companies like the **White Star Line**. Its first White Star ship, **Oceanic**, launched in **1870**, was looked upon as the world's first modern passenger liner, and further orders from **White Star** and other companies like **P & O,** followed. In **1899**, Harland and Wolff delivered the latest White Star ship, **Oceanic II**, then the largest ship afloat, weighing close to 18,000 tons.

For North-East Ulster and Belfast in particular, therefore, the economic link with Britain was absolutely vital. Earlier, religion had been the key factor in distinguishing the North-East from the rest of Ireland, but as the 19th century progressed, this division was reinforced by the economic impact of the Industrial Revolution. While the rest of Ireland remained predominantly agricultural, North-East Ulster was developing as a separate industrial region and consequently was becoming more and more closely linked to industrial Britain. Belfast certainly had much more in common with cities like Glasgow and Manchester than it had with Dublin.

SOURCE **B**

'The industrial revolution in the North-East ... separated Ulster from the rest of Ireland, for the North-East relied mainly on Britain and abroad for markets and raw materials and its industrial structure was ... bound up with that of Britain. The result was that Ulster hardly ever looked southwards and had more in common with Merseyside and Clydeside than with the rest of Ireland.'

From *A History of Northern Ireland* by Patrick Buckland, 1981.

SOURCE C

"By the time of the First Home Rule Bill, the Ulster Protestants felt wedded to the United Kingdom by something much stronger than mere traditional opposition to Catholic Ireland. Their livelihood was wholly bound up with the United Kingdom's prosperity, and any proposal which seemed to tamper with their bonds with it, seemed also to tamper with that prosperity and that livelihood."

From *The Bold Fenian Men* by Robert Kee

SOURCE D

A contemporary postcard

SOURCE E

"To our mind, the progress of Ireland since the Union, and especially since the famine, affords the strongest ... proof that her future should be even more prosperous than her past ... Why should we fear the future now, when we are so much better prepared to meet it?"

From:
The Union Vindicated. Ireland's progress 1782 - 1800 - 1886, a pamphlet published by the *Irish Loyal and Patriotic Union*, 1886.

SOURCE F

"The introduction of Mr. Gladstone's Home Rule Bill was followed by a heavy fall in all Irish securities. In October 1885 the market value was £18,207,000, and in May, after Mr. Gladstone's scheme had been submitted to Parliament, the market value of the same amount ... had fallen to £14,934,000. Since the advent of the Unionist Government however, there had been a gradual recovery, and a considerable portion of what was lost has been regained."

From:
The Economist, 18 May 1889. Reprinted in a leaflet *Home Rule and Irish Securities* by the Irish Unionist Alliance in 1893.

?

1   Study Source **A**. What does it tell us about the feelings of Unionists regarding their links with Britain?

2   Explain why the four provinces in Ireland are called "Prosperity", "Poverty", "Maynooth", and "Land League" provinces.

3   How useful is Source **A** to historians of the period? What other evidence would they need to help them explain Unionist feelings?

4   What can we learn from Source **B** about Ulster's relationship with Britain?

5   Source **D** makes reference to a scene from the Bible, therefore it must be reliable. Explain why you agree or disagree with this.

6   Sources **E** and **F** are written from the point of view of the Unionists and therefore they must be unreliable. Explain why you agree or disagree with this comment.

2.4 Ulster Unionism

The movement to maintain the Union was stirred into action with the introduction of the First Home Rule Bill in 1886. The 1884 Reform Act had trebled the number of Irish voters, and this encouraged the development of both Unionism and Nationalism. Previously, Ulster had returned a number of Liberal MPs, but Gladstone's conversion to Home Rule in 1885 dealt a fatal blow to Ulster Liberalism. In the 1885 general election not a single Liberal candidate was returned as the 103 Irish seats at Westminster were divided between 85 Home Rulers and 18 Conservatives. The Conservatives, nearly all of whom were elected for Ulster constituencies, worked closely with the Orange Order. Like Parnell's Nationalists, they formed a distinctive body in the House of Commons and soon became known as the Ulster Unionists. Their leader was a Co. Cavan landowner, **Colonel E J Saunderson**.

THE 1886 HOME RULE BILL

In January 1886 the Ulster Unionists formed the **Ulster Loyalist Anti-Repeal Union** to organise opposition to Home Rule. This was a significant move, because the new body emphasised Ulster opposition to Home Rule. In the previous year the **Irish Loyal and Patriotic Union** had been set up in Dublin to co-ordinate Home Rule resistance on behalf of all Irish Unionists, but the formation of the Ulster body was an early indication that Unionists in the North-East, where their numbers were substantial, would be prepared to act on their own initiative. Still, these divisions within Unionism were largely overlooked at the time, as Irish Unionists combined with British Conservatives and the 93 Liberals who voted against Gladstone to defeat the First Home Rule Bill.

The introduction of the bill naturally raised tension in Ulster. In June 1886 bitter sectarian trouble erupted in Belfast, and it continued through the summer months into mid-September. Altogether, the 1886 riots claimed about 50 lives, with many others sustaining injuries, and substantial damage to property. For many of the city's inhabitants the political issue of Home Rule was translated into simple religious rivalry, as Catholic and Protestant mobs fought with each other in vicious street battles.

THE ULSTER UNIONIST CONVENTION 1892

The very serious nature of the 1886 rioting, which marked the worst period of violence in 19th century Ireland, alarmed the British government, but Gladstone remained committed to implementing Home Rule. Although calm was restored, the prospect of further violence returned in 1892. To Unionists it appeared likely that Salisbury's government would fall and that Gladstone would introduce a new Home Rule Bill on his return to power. With this in mind Unionists in the North-East organised an **Ulster Unionist Convention** which met in Belfast in **June 1892**.

This turned out to be a very impressive display of Unionist determination to oppose any attempt by a Westminster government to impose Home Rule, and it was now clear that the Unionists were better organised than they had been in 1886. The Convention met at the Botanic Gardens in Belfast, where a special wooden pavilion had been constructed

SOURCE A

Col. Edward Saunderson.

SOURCE B

"Resolution 3 ... we would record our undying allegiance to the gracious monarch who has so long and so wisely wielded the sceptre over the mighty Empire of which Ireland forms an integral part ... our fixed resolve never to submit to laws enacted by an Irish parliament of which the members would be the nominees and puppets of the Roman Priesthood ... "

Resolution for Orange demonstration, 12 July 1893.

SOURCE C

"Since the death of Mr. Parnell, the Irish members are nothing more or less than the delegates of the Irish Roman Catholic priests."

From a speech by Joseph Chamberlain MP, 13 Oct 1891.

to accommodate the 12,000 delegates. The delegates, who came from all over Ulster, represented a wide cross-section of Ulster's Protestant community with approximately one-third of them being tenant farmers. Looking at the 400 strong platform party, however, it was clear that the upper and middle classes would lead opposition to Home Rule. Many of the 400 were either big landowners or prominent businessmen, and the Convention was chaired by the Duke of Abercorn, one of the province's best known landowners.

THE 1893 HOME RULE BILL

Several speakers at the Convention had indicated that if Home Rule was forced on them, then the Ulstermen would resist using any means at their disposal. Yet when Gladstone returned to power a few months later, he ignored these threats of violence and introduced the Second Home Rule Bill. Perhaps one reason why Gladstone refused to be influenced by these dire warnings from Ulster Unionists was that he, like they, knew that even if his measure was successful in the House of Commons, it would be rejected by the huge Conservative majority in the Lords. Therefore, in their struggle against Home Rule, Unionists had two great advantages. One was the clear support of the British Conservative party which, in fact, was to be in power for the 10 years after the 1895 general election. Linked to this was the position of the House of Lords, or upper house as it was known. While it retained its existing powers, which allowed it to **veto** any bill sent up, any further attempt to pass Home Rule would almost certainly be blocked. Thus Nationalist hopes and Unionist fears would ultimately depend on whether the powers of the House of Lords could be reduced.

SOURCE D

'The Convention met in a special wooden pavilion constructed in three weeks on the plains beside the Botanical Gardens, Belfast, on Friday 17 June 1892 ... The main streets were decked with flags and bunting; hotels and all other available accommodation were booked up days beforehand, and crowds poured into the city by every train and steamer.'

The Times, 18 June 1892.

SOURCE E

'One with Great Britain, heart and soul One life, one flag, one fleet, one throne.'

These words of the Poet Laureate appeared above the platform at the Ulster Unionist Convention, 1892.

SOURCE F

THE ASSAULT!!   A *Punch* cartoon of 18 March 1893.

?

1 What impression of Colonel Saunderson is given in Source **A**? How useful is such a photograph to an historian? Explain your answer.

2 Who did the Unionists fear most in the event of Home Rule? (**B** and **C**)

3 What can we learn about the organisation of the Ulster Unionist Convention from Sources **D** and **E**?

4 How is the opposition to Home Rule portrayed in Source **F**? Who is looking out of the fortress window?

5 These sources are all primary. How useful are they to an historian looking at Unionist reaction to the first two Home Rule Bills?

2.5 Southern Unionism

Although the violence associated with opposition to Home Rule was confined to the North-East, Unionists in the rest of Ireland were equally determined to fight any move which interfered with Ireland's existing position within the Union. As we have seen in the 1885 general election, the anti-Home Rulers were a scattered minority in the three southern provinces and carried little political weight outside Dublin. All their candidates in the South, apart from those returned for Trinity College, Dublin, were decisively beaten, and this forced the Southern Unionists to review their tactics. It was clear that as they formed such a small minority, there was really little point in contesting elections against the dominant Home Rule party, and this convinced them that they could be more effective by concentrating their efforts on propaganda. They wanted to persuade others, especially in Britain, that the maintenance of the Union was essential to British, as well as Irish, interests.

THE IRISH UNIONIST ALLIANCE 1891

In 1891 the Irish Loyal and Patriotic Union was re-organised, in an effort to make it more effective, into the **Irish Unionist Alliance**. Although its name suggested that Unionists all over Ireland would now work closely together, the new body represented only Unionists in the South. Initially, the Southern Unionist leaders wanted to establish an all-Ireland body, but they found that Unionists in Ulster were determined to have their own organisation to direct their opposition to Home Rule.

While the numbers involved in the Irish Unionist Alliance were never large, it did achieve a certain degree of success. Its main advantage was money, as most leading Southern Unionists made large financial contributions to the anti-Home Rule publicity campaign. Southern Unionists, of course, were very wealthy. Many were big landowners, while others were important members of the business and professional classes in Dublin and Cork. Indeed some Southern Unionists, notably its two most prominent leaders, **Lord Lansdowne** and **Lord Midleton**, had large estates in Ireland and England, and consequently they were closely connected to the wealthy Conservative establishment in Britain.

Despite their small numbers, therefore, these Unionists exerted great influence in the South. Their wealth had given them a special position in the various local communities, where they were viewed as natural leaders. Southern Unionists also formed a close-knit group frequently marrying within their own circle, which helped them to maintain their prominent positions in Irish society. This exclusive body to which they belonged, and their connections with Britain gave them great confidence and enabled them to function as an effective political group despite their numerical weakness.

Still, these very qualities made Unionists in the South very different from their counterparts in the North-East. Southern Unionists were more closely integrated with British Conservatism, while Ulster Unionists felt less inclined to look outside the province for allies. In North-East Ulster especially, the Unionists' numerical strength allowed them to develop differently. Here the influence of the Orange Order and the fact that it contained elements of all the social classes made Ulster Unionism much more militant, and they were less tolerant of the Catholic religion

SOURCE A

A Southern Unionist leader.

SOURCE B

"(1) To continue, extend and render more efficient the work carried on since May 1885 by the Irish Loyal and Patriotic Union.
 (2) To further consolidate the several Unionist Associations existing in Ireland and
 (3) To establish cordial relations with the Unionist Associations that have been formed in England and Scotland."

Preamble to the constitution of the *Irish Unionist Alliance* (previously the *Irish Loyal and Patriotic Union*) 8 April 1891.

SOURCE C

"I have talked to Col. Rowan ... and he thinks with me that it will be almost impossible to get a conference together. Moreover, those who would attend a conference are not persons who will be inclined to work, rather those who come because others come, so they are ashamed to remain at home ... In Kerry there are so few who will take any trouble, or do anything unless they are paid for working."

Letter from Miss A.M. Rowan, Tralee, Co. Kerry, to the secretary of the Irish Unionist Alliance, 15 Oct 1892.

SOURCE D

> "I called a meeting for the purpose of forming a club and got together a good many after a time, but numbers do not understand the movement. They are simply like a flock of sheep without a shepherd to lead them ... We can do nothing against Home Rule without men thoroughly organised on the club system."

Speech by Sir Augustus Warren, Co. Cork, to a meeting of the Unionist Clubs Council in Belfast, 2 May 1893.

than Southern Unionists. This was not surprising, because the Southern Unionists' lack of numbers made them more dependent on local Catholics whom they employed as tradesmen, farm labourers, servants, etc. This tended not to happen in Ulster. Equally, their lack of numbers meant that the option of using violence in their opposition to Home Rule was never seriously contemplated in the South, whereas the numerical superiority of Ulster Unionists encouraged them to consider a more extreme course of action.

SOUTHERN UNIONISTS IN THE LORDS

It would be wrong , therefore, to dismiss the Southern Unionists as only fringe players in the struggle against Home Rule, as their electoral performance in 1885 had indicated. In fact, about a dozen Southern Unionist MPs later took refuge in safe English seats and continued to highlight their case in the House of Commons. The Southern Unionists were also well represented in the House of Lords, where over 80 of the 100 Irish peers were Southern Unionists. This gave them a base from which they could operate and use their connections to influence the Conservative party. Indeed, it may be more accurate to speak of prominent Southern Unionists, such as Lansdowne and Midleton, as leaders not just of Irish, but of British Unionism.

SOURCE G

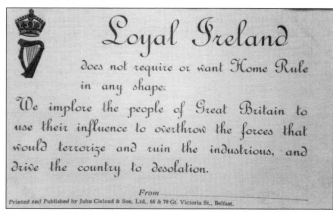

Postcards like these were signed and then posted to friends in Great Britain.

SOURCE E

> "Since March [1892] three millions of leaflets dealing with various phases of the question have been scattered broadcast by them throughout England, Ireland, Scotland and Wales. At present the committee is engaged distributing 250,000 pamphlets in advocacy [support] of the Union through the various polling districts of Lancashire."

Irish Unionist Alliance Report, 1893.

SOURCE F

> "In the year 1895 ... Lord Salisbury and the Duke of Devonshire publically thanked the Alliance for its services in helping to return that Government to power ... The Government conceives itself to have no further use for those Irish Unionists whose efforts turned the scale in its favour in 1895..."

Dublin *Daily Express*, 31 May 1900.

1 What evidence is there in this section to support the view that the Southern Unionists had contacts with and influence over groups in other parts of the United Kingdom? (**B**, **E**,**F**,**G** and **T**)

2 What reasons are given for the failure to form active Unionist Clubs in the South? (**C** and **D**)

3 What were the aims of the Irish Unionist Alliance? (**B** and **T**)

4 How and why did the English Government's attitude to the Southern Unionists appear to change between 1895 and 1900? (**F** and **T**)

2.6 Irish Unionists and British Conservatives

Home Rule was such a contentious issue, because it divided British, as well as Irish, politics. Hence, British Liberals lined up with Irish Nationalists to oppose British Conservatives and Irish Unionists. While Gladstone was a passionate believer in the need to grant Home Rule if lasting peace and good relations were to exist between Britain and Ireland, British Conservatives were equally committed in their opposition to Home Rule. The Conservative party had always been closely identified with the British Empire. They saw the extension of British power over great parts of the world as something that was good for the people in these countries, as they believed that by controlling countries such as India they were providing a civilising influence on a basically backward native population. Of course, they expected and received considerable financial rewards for the improvements they claimed they were making by the way of cheap raw materials, which were shipped from all over the Empire for the benefit of British industry.

THE CONSERVATIVES AND HOME RULE

When they looked at the question of Home Rule, Conservatives regarded it not just as an Irish, but an imperial issue. They were certain that any move which conferred even a small measure of political freedom on Ireland would open the floodgates, and lead to a series of demands from around the Empire for similar concessions. Ultimately, they believed that this would result in the break-up of the British Empire, and they were determined to prevent it. The adoption of the title **Unionist** by English Conservatives after 1886 shows the level of their commitment to the defence of the Union. It is, therefore, correct to talk about **British Unionism** in this period. British Unionists were united with Ulster Unionists and Southern Unionists in their opposition to Home Rule, though differences later emerged on the precise methods each group would use in undertaking this opposition.

As we noted earlier, the 1893 Home Rule Bill was very similar to the First Home Rule Bill, and similar arguments were presented for and against the measure on each occasion. The main Unionist argument was that Home Rule would only be the first step on the road to complete separation, and the bill, therefore, would only be a temporary or stop-gap measure leading inevitably to complete independence. Naturally, the Home Rule party rejected this, claiming that Home Rule was the absolute limit of their wishes or aspirations, and arguing that they regarded it as a permanent settlement of the Irish Question. Neither the British nor the Irish Unionists were convinced by these assurances. To some Conservatives the appeals made by both Southern and Ulster Unionists that they were loyal citizens of the Crown, and simply wanted to continue as such, was a powerful influence, persuading many that Unionists in Ireland should not be abandoned.

'ULSTER WILL FIGHT'

It must also be true that at the beginning of 1886, when the Liberal party adopted Home Rule, the Conservatives saw an opportunity to divide and discredit their opponents by coming out strongly against the measure. The key figure in this was the colourful Conservative peer, **Lord Randolph Churchill**. In February 1886 Churchill visited Belfast on

SOURCE A

'Though in 1886 Irish Conservatives had hung up cartoons of Gladstone and Parnell in their lavatories, other Irish Unionists, especially in Ulster, had been Liberals ... However, the Liberal leader's refusal to accept the views of Irish Unionists ... broke finally the spell of Gladstone's personality and underlined the futility of hoping for any favourable consideration from the Liberal Party.'

From *Irish Unionism 1885-1923*, by Patrick Buckland, 1973.

SOURCE B

'My dear Montgomery - I quite agree with you that we must subordinate any opinions of our own to those of Chamberlain ...

But it is really hard to keep one's temper. In his Clapham speech, he rails against Catholics and shows me clearly what an intolerant man he is. We don't care to have our religious emblems spoken of as 'so called' religious emblems. I am sorely tempted to give him the rough side of my tongue over this and I am not sure that I won't.

Sincerely yours,

W. Kenny.'

Letter to H de F Montgomery 26 Oct 1894

SOURCE C

'Conservatives and Unionists in Britain, as well as those in Ireland, completely rejected the notion of Home Rule ... They feared that any such concession at a time when other European states were accumulating overseas empires would spark off a chain reaction and lead to the eventual break-up of the British Empire.'

From *A History of Northern Ireland* by Patrick Buckland, 1981.

Saunderson's invitation, and he informed an excited audience that the Conservative party would stand by the Unionists in their hour of need. In doing so Churchill was identifying the Conservative party with Unionist, particularly Ulster Unionist, resistance to Home Rule. Later, he gave encouragement to militant Unionists in the province, when he uttered his famous phrase, **'Ulster will fight and Ulster will be right'.** This inspired the Ulstermen to take their resistance to any lengths, even if it meant using force, and laid the foundation for a close alliance between the Conservatives and Ulster Unionists, an alliance which was to become even stronger in the critical years after 1910.

KILLING HOME RULE WITH KINDNESS

The scale of the defeat for the Second Home Rule Bill in the House of Lords, 419 votes to 41, gave a clear indication of the Conservative party's total opposition to Home Rule. Yet when the Conservatives began an unbroken 10 years in government in 1895, they approached the Irish Question with a great deal of caution. Gone was the wild talk of resisting Home Rule by whatever means possible. In its place was the carefully thought-out strategy of **Killing Home Rule with Kindness**.

SOURCE F

Neighbour- *"Where are ye drivin' him to Johnny?"*

Redmond- *"Whisht, ye Divil ye! It's Home Rule he thinks we're goin' to; but its Separation I'm drivin' him to."*

SOURCE D

'I decided some time ago that if [Gladstone] went for Home Rule, the Orange card was the one to play.'

Lord Randolph Churchill, Feb 1886.

SOURCE E

'To summarise the results of this visit to England, I would say that the deepest interest is taken in our organisation, and it is understood as representing the existence of the fixed determination of the Loyalists in Ireland never to submit to Home Rule... I had numerous opportunities for consultation with men of political influence, and I was glad to find that the best thought in Ireland was quite in line with all that is more essential to the Unionist cause in Great Britain.'

Report by Viscount Templetown of his visit to England to publicise the Unionist Clubs, June 1893.

1   What reasons are given in Sources **B** and **C** to explain why British Conservatives opposed Home Rule?

2   What are the strengths and weaknesses of using only Unionist accounts of the Home Rule issue? (**B**,**D** and **E**)

3   In what ways would the views of an Irish Unionist and a British Conservative (Unionist) be (a) similar (b) different ? (see **T** and also pages **28-31**)

4   What evidence is there in Source **F** that Home Rule was not enough for many Nationalists?

3.1 The Constitutional Crisis and the 1910 Elections

The Conservative defeat in the general election of January 1906 sent them out of government for a long period. The new Liberal government was led by **Sir Henry Campbell-Bannerman**, and his Cabinet included a number of high calibre ministers such as David Lloyd George, Winston Churchill and H H Asquith. In fact **Asquith** became Prime Minister when Campbell-Bannerman retired in April 1908. As the Liberals had won a landslide victory in the general election, they had a large majority in the House of Commons and did not depend on the Home Rule party for support. By this time the Home Rule party was usually referred to as the **Irish Parliamentary Party (IPP)**. Ten years after the Parnellite split it had reunited under a new leader, **John Redmond**. The main consequence of these changes, as far as Ireland was concerned, was that there was no possibility of a new Home Rule Bill being introduced in the immediate future. These were disappointing years for Redmond and the IPP, because they could make little impact on British politics. Their only strategy was to wait patiently until the Liberals again required their support.

THE ULSTER UNIONIST COUNCIL 1905

For the Unionists the fact that Home Rule was off the agenda meant that they could relax in the knowledge that no real change was imminent. An earlier scare concerning a modified form of Home Rule had led to the formation of a new Ulster group, the **Ulster Unionist Council**, which came into existence in **March 1905**. This new body further emphasised the differences between Ulster and Southern Unionists, and it was to play a crucial role in directing Ulster resistance to Home Rule in the years ahead. It was clear from this point on that no matter what path the Southern Unionists might follow, the Ulster Unionists would be the main opponents of Home Rule, and, if necessary, they would carry on this resistance on their own. Still, after 1906 they had little need to worry about organising opposition, as the Liberal government became increasingly pre-occupied with other political issues.

THE PEOPLE'S BUDGET 1909

Circumstances were to change dramatically with the defeat of the 1909 Budget in the House of Lords. This measure had been introduced by the Chancellor, Lloyd George, who wanted to raise extra money to

SOURCE **A**

A contemporary postcard depicting John Redmond. The portrait of Redmond was in the form of a flap which lifted to reveal a strip of photographs showing prominent Nationalist politicians. The same firm produced a similar card showing Carson and Unionist politicians.

provide help for the poorest sections of society, such as the old and the unemployed. To do this he proposed to introduce a new tax on the rich, but his scheme was fiercely opposed by the Conservative party, particularly in the House of Lords, where the People's Budget, as it became known, was rejected by the Conservative majority there. This created a great controversy, known as the **constitutional crisis**, over whether the House of Commons, which was elected, should have more control than the House of Lords, which was not elected.

THE 1910 ELECTIONS

Asquith called a general election on the issue. The result of the **January 1910 election**, however, was inconclusive. The Liberals won 275 seats, the Unionists (British Conservatives and Irish Unionists together) 273, Irish Nationalists 82 and Labour 40. Subsequent efforts to resolve the constitutional crisis by negotiations between the party leaders also failed, and another election was called in **December 1910**. The results of this second general election were equally inconclusive. The Liberals now had 272 seats, exactly the same as the Unionists, while the Irish Nationalists won 84 and Labour 42. Asquith remained as leader of the Liberal government, but the figures reveal that he was now dependent on the Irish Nationalists for support. It appeared, therefore, that Redmond's strategy of waiting until the Liberals needed Irish support to stay in power had finally paid off.

THE PARLIAMENT ACT 1911

The way was now open for a simple deal. If the Irish MPs would support a new bill to reduce the powers of the House of Lords, Asquith could introduce a Third Home Rule Bill. Of course, the two were connected, because any new Home Rule Bill would have to find a way through the Lords. Consequently, Redmond must have been delighted to organise IPP support for the **Parliament Act**, which became law in **August 1911**. The new act reduced the veto powers of the House of Lords. From this point on any bill opposed by the Lords could only be delayed for a period of two years, after which it could become law. If, therefore, the Liberals remained in power, the passage of a Home Rule Act seemed certain.

SOURCE B

"Throughout the crisis, Irish support for the Liberals in the House of Commons had been the decisive factor, and the implications for Home Rule of the abolition of the Lord's veto had never been far from Irish Nationalists' minds."

From *The Bold Fenian Men* by Robert Kee, 1972.

SOURCE C

"The year 1910 marked the closing of a chapter in the history of the Irish Parliamentary Party. Redmond's policy of fostering the Liberal alliance had at last succeeded."

From *Home Rule and the Irish Question* by Grenfell Morton, 1980.

SOURCE D

"Its objects shall be to form an Ulster Union for bringing into line all local Unionist Associations in the Province of Ulster ... to act as a further connecting link between Ulster Unionists and their parliamentary representatives ... to express Ulster Unionist opinion ..."

Extracts from the agenda of a meeting on 2 December 1904 to set up the Ulster Unionist Council.

SOURCE E

"What I am really anxious about is to satisfy myself that the people over there [Ulster] really mean to resist ... Personally I would be prepared to make any sacrifice, my time, business, money, or even my liberty, if I felt assured we would not in the end be abandoned."

Letter from Sir Edward Carson to James Craig, 29 July 1911.

1 Place the events mentioned in this section between 1905 and 1911 in chronological order.

2 What effects had Irish Nationalist support for the Liberals had on the Home Rule issue? (**B** and **C**)

3 Study Source **D**. What does it tell you about the relationship between Ulster and Southern Unionists in 1904?

4 In Source **E** what did Carson hope his personal sacrifices would prove?

3.2 The Third Home Rule Bill

Asquith introduced the **Third Home Rule Bill** in the House of Commons on **11 April 1912**. The new bill was practically the same as the **1886** and **1893** bills, which meant that the proposed new parliament in Dublin would be restricted to dealing with internal affairs only, while many important matters would continue to be under Westminster's control. In addition, Asquith gave repeated assurances that the Westminster parliament or imperial parliament would retain total supremacy over the Irish parliament, which meant, in effect, that any bill passed in Dublin but not meeting Westminster's approval could be rejected. This was unlikely to please Irish Nationalists, but at the time Redmond and his colleagues played down the negative side of the bill, while arguing that the measure, as it stood, would go far enough to satisfy Irish aspirations. Unionists, however, refused to believe these pledges. They steadfastly maintained that Home Rule would be the first step on the road to full independence.

Even before the introduction of the Third Home Rule Bill the Unionists had launched their campaign of resistance. In Britain there were cries that the Liberal government was acting unconstitutionally because there had been no mention of any new Home Rule Bill in the party's manifesto for the second general election in 1910. It was also claimed that the Asquith-Redmond deal was a conspiracy to exclude loyal citizens from the British Empire. Certainly, there was some justification in the argument that the question of Home Rule had not been properly submitted to the voters in 1910, because Asquith and the other Liberal leaders had been careful to avoid any mention of the issue during the election campaign. On the other hand the Conservatives had made Home Rule a key issue, as practically all of their candidates had linked the Lords' crisis to the Home Rule question. Therefore, voters in Britain were fully aware of the implications for Home Rule if the Liberal party was returned to government.

ASQUITH AND THE NATIONALISTS

Yet in some ways the link between the Liberal party and the Irish Nationalists was not quite as strong as it had been in the latter part of the 19th century. For one thing Asquith was not committed to the principle of Home Rule in the way that Gladstone had been. To Asquith the introduction of a new Home Rule Bill was simply a debt that had to be repaid. The Irish MPs had supported his

SOURCE A

A contemporary postcard.

SOURCE B

A contemporary postcard.

government at a critical phase, and he was going to reward them with the Home Rule measure that they had been seeking for so long. It is extremely doubtful, however, that he would ever have taken the risk of introducing Home Rule, if he had not required the IPP's support. In this sense he was, as Unionists claimed, Redmond's prisoner.

BONAR LAW AND THE UNIONISTS

Meanwhile, the link between British Conservatives and Irish Unionists was strengthened by a new development. When the moderate **Balfour** resigned as Conservative party leader in 1911, **Andrew Bonar Law** emerged as the party's surprise choice to succeed him. Stung by the two election reverses in 1910 Bonar Law was determined that the Conservative/Unionist party should go the offensive. The party had been out of power since the end of 1905 and had become divided, as leading members quarrelled among themselves over different items of policy. Bonar Law's task was to unite the party. To do this he chose the one issue which he knew would have the total support of his party, and this was absolute opposition to any form of Home Rule. Recognising that Asquith was relatively weak on this crucial question, Bonar Law was determined to exploit the issue for the benefit of his party. There was yet another factor which contributed to Bonar Law's determination to prevent Home Rule. He was a Scotsman of Ulster descent, who retained close links with the province. This meant that he could both identify with and understand Ulster resistance to Home Rule better than most of his Conservative colleagues. With Bonar Law as Conservative leader the Ulster Unionists were assured of unswerving support for their cause.

SOURCE C

> "I said earlier it is impossible to grant Home Rule. The opposition of Ulster ... makes it impossible ... I was present last week at a gathering of the [Ulster Unionists at Belfast] ... It was the expression of the soul of a people. They say they will not submit, except by force to such a government."

Speech in the House of Commons by Bonar Law, 16 April 1912.

SOURCE D

CARSON - "Take it away, it smells; been buried twice already; bury it again, this time *for good*."

?

1 In Source **A**, who is represented by (a) the policeman (b) the man in the carriage? (**T**)

2 The large hand on the policeman is coloured red in the postcard. What is the significance of this?

3 Cartoons and postcards such as Sources **A**,**B** and **D** provide evidence which is of only limited value to an historian. Explain why you agree or disagree with this statement.

4 What can we learn from Source **C** about the apparent strength of feeling in Ulster about the Home Rule issue?

5 How reliable is a source such as **C**? Explain your answer.

6 Using Sources **B**,**C** and **D**, what can we learn about Unionist reactions to the Home Rule Bill?

3.3 Resistance to Home Rule

SOURCE A

Sir James Craig's private residence at Craigavon, Co. Down.

SOURCE B

"We must be prepared, in the event of a Home Rule Bill passing, with such measures as will carry on for ourselves the government of those districts of which we have control. We must be prepared ... the morning Home Rule passes, ourselves to become responsible for the government of the Protestant Province of Ulster. ... Our motto is 'We rely on ourselves.'"

Speech by Sir Edward Carson to a Unionist rally at Craig's home, 23 September 1911.

As expected, opposition to the Third Home Rule Bill was centred on Ulster. During the early parliamentary debates on the new bill most leading Unionist speakers raised the question of Ulster. In general, they claimed that there were two different sets of people in Ireland. Not only were there two religions, there were **two races** or even **two nations** in the country. For the Unionists it followed that if Ireland was entitled to Home Rule, then Ulster was equally entitled to special treatment. Some MPs actually raised the possibility of **Home Rule within Home Rule**, but this was immediately rejected by Asquith. Still, in these early debates it was noticeable that Liberal government spokesmen were keen to avoid the question of Ulster. Indeed, little attention had been paid to the Ulster problem in the cabinet discussions leading up the the bill's introduction.

SIR EDWARD CARSON

In 1912 the Unionists had a clear objective. This was not to win special treatment for Ulster, but to use the Ulster question to force the government to withdraw the measure altogether. Of great benefit to the Ulster Unionists at this time was the performance of their leader. In February 1910, **Sir Edward Carson**, a Dublin-born lawyer, had become leader of the Ulster Unionists. In one way Carson was a strange choice to lead the Ulstermen, because he was a **Southern Unionist** who lived in London, where he had a very successful legal practice. Yet Carson turned out to be an inspiring leader of Ulster Unionism. He had considerable intellectual ability, and this coupled with his fierce determination and coolness in the face of crisis made him a formidable politician. He was also a brilliant orator who could rouse large audiences with passionate speeches, and he had a marvellous sense of drama which he frequently used to great effect. An early indication of his speaking ability came in September 1911, when he addressed 50,000 Orangemen outside Belfast at the home of **Sir James Craig**. This was an event of crucial importance, and it set the tone for future opposition to Home Rule.

SOURCE C

"I said to him [Churchill] that most certainly the moment the Home Rule Bill was passed you would not only set up your own provisional government, but that you would allow no force of any kind in your area except the force appointed by you; that you would appoint your own police and allow no other body to interfere with your action."

Letter from Bonar Law to Sir Edward Carson, 18 Sept 1913.

SOURCE D

"They may, perhaps they will, carry their Home Rule Bill through the House of Commons, but what then? I said the other day in the House of Commons and I repeat here that there are things stronger than parliamentary majorities."

Speech by Bonar Law at Blenheim Palace, England, July 1912.

SIR JAMES CRAIG

Earlier, Carson had written to Craig warning him that resistance to Home Rule would entail great sacrifices on the part of the Ulster population. To assure Carson that he could count on the unflinching support of the Ulster Protestants, Craig had organised this great demonstration at **Craigavon**, his home on the shores of Belfast Lough. Craig was very different from Carson. Quiet and unassuming, he nevertheless demonstrated excellent organising ability and the cool head necessary for his role as Carson's lieutenant. The two men seemed to complement each other perfectly, and together they provided the Ulster Unionists with the resolute and inspirational leadership, which the situation demanded.

SOURCE E

A group of prominent Unionists at Craigavon (Sir James Craig's home). Behind them is the famous conservatory.

PROTEST MEETINGS

Mass protest meetings, like the one at Craigavon, became a central feature of the Unionist resistance campaign, and Craig used the existing structure of the Orange Order to make the necessary arrangements for such demonstrations. Perhaps the most important of these took place at **Balmoral**, on the outskirts of Belfast, on 9 April 1912, just two days before Asquith introduced the Third Home Rule Bill. This demonstration attracted a crowd of 100,000, many of whom had obviously been practising military-style drilling in the previous weeks. On this occasion the third member of the Unionist opposition triangle, **Bonar Law**, addressed the huge crowd, emphasising the wider aspect of British Unionism, when he described Ulster as 'the key to the Empire'. Indeed Bonar Law went further at another impressive gathering, this time at **Blenheim Palace** in the south of England, when he publicly warned the Liberal government that there were 'things stronger than parliamentary majorities'. He developed this line of attack by declaring Conservative party support for any Ulster act of resistance, including the resort to force. This type of language by politicians had not been heard since the Cromwellian period in the 17th century, and it was a direct threat to Asquith and his colleagues. While they condemned these wild speeches, the Liberals refused to offer any concessions to the Unionists. The prospect of drastic action in Ulster appeared closer as each week passed.

?

1   How might the speeches made by Carson and Bonar Law have been influenced by the fact that they were addressing large crowds of Unionists? (**B**,**D** and **T**)

2   Why were the Ulster Unionists contemplating setting up a government of their own? (**B** and **C**)

3   What class of people do the Unionist leaders shown in Source **E** appear to be?

4   What are the strengths and weaknesses of using only Source **E** to describe the prominent Unionists of the time?

3.4 Propaganda

In the struggle to present their case and influence others, both Unionists and Nationalists produced a vast quantity of propaganda material. These appeared in the form of posters, newspaper advertisements, labels, pamphlets and postcards, all of which were considered useful in spreading views in the days before television and radio. If a political message could be conveyed in an amusing cartoon, it often attracted extra publicity, and this was obviously considered an advantage by the leaders of both parties.

SOURCE A

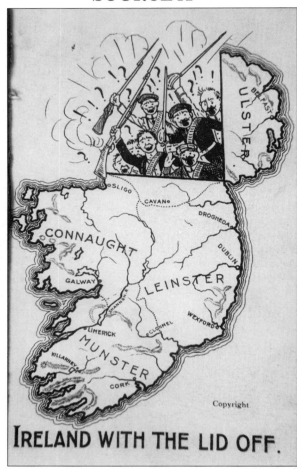

IRELAND WITH THE LID OFF.

SOURCE B

AGAINST HOME RULE HANDS UP!

SOURCE C

The HOME RULE ROUT

SOURCE D

SOURCE E

SOURCE F

SOURCE G

?

1   What does Source **B** tell us about the number of Ulster counties opposing Home Rule?

2   How is life under Home Rule portrayed in Source **D**?

3   Sources **A**, **C** and **G** are cartoons. Are they reliable as evidence? Explain your answer.

4   Sources **E** and **F** are pro-Home Rule propaganda. How do these sources portray their views?

5   Is Source **G** pro or anti-Home Rule? Explain your answer. See the rear cover where this postcard appears in colour.

6   What other forms of evidence would you require to give you a full picture of the views held by Unionists and Nationalists at this time?

3.5 The Ulster Covenant

The events of the first part of 1912 had shown that Unionist resistance to Home Rule would not be confined to the House of Commons. Outside Parliament, the Ulster Protestant population had been stirred into action. Numbers joining the Orange Order were on the increase, and attendances at public meetings to voice criticism of Home Rule were high. Not surprisingly, in Belfast, where religious rivalry was never far from the surface, the events of 1912 saw a new wave of sectarian rioting. As the Home Rule Bill progressed through parliament, tension in Ulster, already inflamed by speeches from Carson and other leading Unionists, reached fever pitch. The prospect of Protestant mob violence alarmed Craig who realised that Ulster resistance would only be successful if it was controlled and directed by the leadership. What the campaign required was something which could give Ulster Protestants a focus and also win further sympathy for the Unionist cause in Britain.

ULSTER DAY 28 SEPTEMBER 1912

To achieve this Craig hit on the idea of a **Solemn League and Covenant** for Ulster. This proved to be a propaganda master stroke. The plan was that as many citizens as possible would sign a copy of the Covenant during a week of packed activity in September 1912. Audiences all over the North were addressed by Carson, Craig and a number of other leading Unionists from England and Ireland, and the week ended with an emotional demonstration on Saturday 28 September. This was called **Ulster Day**. Carson himself signed the Covenant in Belfast's City Hall with a silver pen presented specially for the occasion. He was followed by the rest of the Unionist leadership. All over the province there were centres for people to record their signatures. To show their determination many actually signed in their own blood. When the figures were added up, over 450,000 men and women signed the Covenant. The day was considered a great success. Journalists from England informed their readers of the solemn occasion, and reported the determined mood and obvious commitment of the Ulster Protestants. The propaganda objective had thus been achieved.

SOURCE A

Ulster's Solemn League and Covenant.

Being convinced in our consciences that Home Rule would be disastrous to the material well-being of Ulster as well as of the whole of Ireland, subversive of our civil and religious freedom, destructive of our citizenship and perilous to the unity of the Empire, we, whose names are underwritten, men of Ulster, loyal subjects of His Gracious Majesty King George V., humbly relying on the God whom our fathers in days of stress and trial confidently trusted, do hereby pledge ourselves in solemn Covenant throughout this our time of threatened calamity to stand by one another in defending for ourselves and our children our cherished position of equal citizenship in the United Kingdom and in using all means which may be found necessary to defeat the present conspiracy to set up a Home Rule Parliament in Ireland. ¶ And in the event of such a Parliament being forced upon us we further solemnly and mutually pledge ourselves to refuse to recognise its authority. ¶ In sure confidence that God will defend the right we hereto subscribe our names. ¶ And further, we individually declare that we have not already signed this Covenant.

The above was signed by me at *Mount Joy* "Ulster Day." Saturday, 28th September, 1912.

David McFarland

── **God Save the King.** ──

SOURCE B

Carson, Craig and South Londonderry Unionists, at Moneymore.

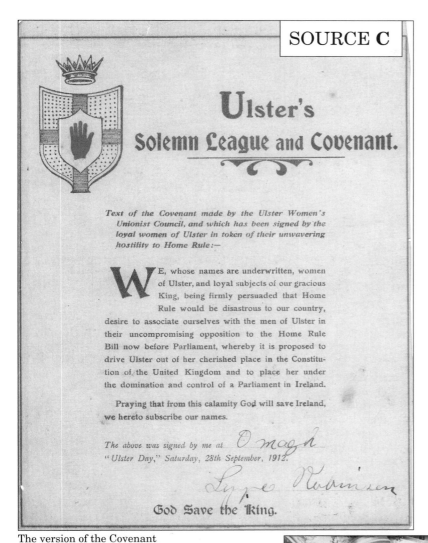

SOURCE C

Ulster's Solemn League and Covenant.

Text of the Covenant made by the Ulster Women's Unionist Council, and which has been signed by the loyal women of Ulster in token of their unwavering hostility to Home Rule:—

WE, whose names are underwritten, women of Ulster, and loyal subjects of our gracious King, being firmly persuaded that Home Rule would be disastrous to our country, desire to associate ourselves with the men of Ulster in their uncompromising opposition to the Home Rule Bill now before Parliament, whereby it is proposed to drive Ulster out of her cherished place in the Constitution of the United Kingdom and to place her under the domination and control of a Parliament in Ireland.

Praying that from this calamity God will save Ireland, we hereto subscribe our names.

The above was signed by me at *Omagh* "Ulster Day," Saturday, 28th September, 1912.

God Save the King.

The version of the Covenant signed by Unionist women

SOURCE D

"After religious services in the churches, in which the hymn 'O God our help in ages past' epitomised the air of crisis, a procession headed by Carson and the faded yellow silk banner, said to have been William III's at the Battle of the Boyne, marched through the streets to Belfast Town Hall, escorted by a guard of honour of 2500 men in bowler hats, carrying walking sticks."

From *The Bold Fenian Men* by Robert Kee, 1972.

?

1   Use all the information provided in this section to write a detailed report of the events of Covenant Day for a newspaper of the time.

SOURCE E

ULSTER DAY. Sir Edward Carson signing the Covenant, Belfast City Hall, 28th Sept 1912.

3.6   The Ulster Volunteers

SOURCE A

Ulster Volunteers on parade at a UVF training camp, Baronscourt, Co. Tyrone. Baronscourt was the home of the Duke of Abercorn, a prominent Unionist.

SOURCE B

"I, Roger Hall, being the commander of the 2nd Battalion, South Down Regiment of the ULSTER VOLUNTEER FORCE, ... apply to you for lawful authority to hold meetings for the purpose of training and drilling..."

"We, being two Justices of the Peace in and for Co. Down hereby give to the members of the above 2nd Battn. S. Down Regt, the authority for which application is above made, and authorise them to act accordingly thereunder.
  16th day of December 1913.
                E. Pedlow J.P.
                J.E. Connor J.P."

Justice's Certificate, issued 16 December 1913.

Towards the end of 1912 an increasing amount of discussion had centred on the exclusion of a number of Ulster counties from the Home Rule Bill. The covenant referred to the historic province of Ulster which meant nine counties, but an amendment to the Home Rule Bill, introduced by a Liberal backbencher as early as June 1912, suggested that the four 'plantation counties', **Antrim, Down, Londonderry and Armagh**, could be left out. Although Asquith maintained that the bill would not be altered and Home Rule would be introduced for the whole of Ireland, it began to look as if some form of exclusion for all or part of Ulster might be the only compromise which could prevent bloodshed. Certainly, Bonar Law and the Conservative party would have backed such a scheme. As the situation developed, Carson reluctantly accepted that his original intention of using Ulster to defeat Home Rule altogether could not succeed, and the best he could hope for was the exclusion of a number of Ulster counties. The question now was, how many counties?

THE ULSTER VOLUNTEERS

Naturally, Redmond was totally opposed to any solution which would divide Ireland in two, and it appeared to the Unionist leadership that he still exerted considerable influence on Asquith. Therefore, resistance had to be stepped up, and to strengthen their position the Ulster Unionist Council decided in **January 1913** to raise an **Ulster Volunteer Force (UVF)** of 100,000 men. It was to be organised on a county basis and recruiting began immediately. Drilling was practised in Orange Halls all over the province, and for most of the UVF men this involved the use of dummy wooden rifles as real weapons were

SOURCE C

Sir Edward Carson acknowledging the cheers of the UVF at Glencairn, near Belfast.

not available. To Redmond and the Nationalists the sight of men marching with dummy rifles was nothing more than a joke, and they viewed the UVF as part of a ploy by Carson to pressurise the Liberal government into making concessions. Initially, Asquith was equally convinced that Carson's threat of force was really only bluff, and he allowed the situation to drift. Yet despite nationalist taunts, the UVF was clearly a menace which the government would have to confront.

UVF TRAINING

The Unionists had announced that the UVF was an armed force which would be used against the government if it tried to force Home Rule on Ulster. To help with its training and organisation leading Unionists had used their contacts in the British Army to recruit experienced officers for the new force. In July 1913 a retired English general, **Sir George Richardson**, arrived in Belfast to take command of the UVF. Beneath him was a very efficient Headquarters Staff which included other officers with long experience in the British Army. Manoeuvres were organised on the large estates all over the province, and the UVF soon appeared as a very determined and efficient force. The one ingredient missing was weapons, but the Unionist leadership was already engaged in organising funds for the purchase of a very large shipment of arms.

SOURCE D

A contemporary postcard.

SOURCE E

"I quite understand that Unionist politicians would very much like to be able to assert in their speeches that the Volunteers will undoubtedly come out and fight at the first attempt to administer the Home Rule Act, but I venture to express a strong hope that this assertion will not be made or encouraged by the leaders of the Unionist Party ..."

Letter from Lord Dunleath to Sir Edward Carson, 9 March 1915.

SOURCE F

"There will be a special parade of the Company, on Friday evening 17th inst., at 8 pm. Full equipment to be worn by every man on parade, including bandolier, belt, haversack, and putties.

Every man on parade will be supplied with a fixed bayonet on this occasion.

Commencing Saturday next at 6 pm every man is to attend Narrow Water shooting range and fire five rounds of the new Mauser rifle."

Orders issued by B. J. Glenny, Warrenpoint Company Commander, UVF, 14 July 1914.

?

1   How can we tell from Sources **A**, **B** and **C** that Ulster Volunteer activity was acceptable to the country's leadership at that time?

2   How does the flag (Source **D**) reinforce the UVF's desire to remain part of the United Kingdom?

3   **(a)** How would you explain the views held by Lord Dunleath in Source **E** regarding the activities of the UVF?
    (b) How is this view contradicted by the orders given in Source **F**?

3.7 The Irish Volunteers

SOURCE A

SOURCE A

A well turned out company of Irish Volunteers, near Strabane, Co. Tyrone.

By the autumn of 1913 it should have been clear to Redmond that cracks were beginning to appear in the Liberal government's Home Rule strategy. While Asquith maintained that no change would be made to the bill, other leading Liberals, notably Churchill and Lloyd George, were of the opinion that Ulster would have to be treated separately. A series of meetings between the party leaders took place from October to December 1913, at which the possible exclusion of some Ulster counties was discussed, but Redmond insisted that Ireland must be treated as a single unit. It looks as if Asquith did not reveal the full extent of his Cabinet's concern over Ulster to the Irish leader. In these circumstances Redmond remained convinced at the end of 1913 that the Liberal government's nerve would hold and special treatment for Ulster would be rejected.

FORMATION OF THE IRISH VOLUNTEERS

Other Nationalists in Ireland, however, did not share Redmond's optimism. They had watched events in Ulster and had witnessed how a well organised body, such as the UVF, could put pressure on the British government. What was required, they insisted, was a similar force in the South, which would ensure that Irish Nationalists would not be betrayed by the Asquith government on the Home Rule question. To these people the one clear fact to emerge from this crisis was that the Liberal government would only respond to force, or at least to the threat of force. The central figure in this new thinking was **Eoin MacNeill**, a well known Dublin academic, who along with Douglas Hyde had founded the Gaelic League in 1893. Under his leadership plans were completed in **November 1913** for the formation of a force of **Irish**

SOURCE B

'By far the most important characteristic of the Irish Volunteers was something quite unknown, not only to the public at large in Ireland ... but also unknown to the majority of the Irish Volunteers themselves. This was the fact that they were secretly under the control of that small group of young men who ... had recently been re-animating the near defunct Irish Republican Brotherhood.'

From *The Bold Fenian Men* by Robert Kee, 1972.

SOURCE C

'The Belfast Volunteers had organised a special train to take a crowd to Dublin for the funeral and we jumped at the chance to get away from the 'loyal' atmosphere of Belfast.'

A Belfast member of *Cumann na mBan* (The Women's Auxiliary Movement), describing the funeral of O'Donovan Rossa, 15 Aug 1915.

Volunteers. Initially, recruitment for the new force was slow, but by the summer of 1914 well over 100,000 men had joined, making it even bigger than the UVF.

REDMOND AND THE IVF

The appearance of this new force in the South, which was really a mirror-image of the UVF in the North, greatly alarmed Redmond. Although MacNeill assured him that the Irish Volunteers would not weaken the IPP, their formation was an indication that a growing number of Irishmen were unhappy with the very moderate line which Redmond was following. As the number of recruits rose rapidly after the spring of 1914, Redmond realised he had to bring the movement under his personal control, something which he tried to accomplish by forcing MacNeill to change the membership of the committee controlling the Irish Volunteers. Redmond had good reason to be concerned, because from the outset a number of violent Nationalists had taken the opportunity to join the Volunteers, hoping to use the movement for their own purpose later on. These were the members of the old Fenian group, or **Irish Republican Brotherhood** (**IRB**) as it was now known, and they were secretly active within the Irish Volunteers.

SOURCE D

Irish Volunteer cavalry at Strabane, 1914.

SOURCE E

"[MacNeill] praised the Ulster Volunteers for their courage, and urged the Home Rulers to form a volunteer force to make sure that the British Government kept its promise to grant Home Rule. The IRB had been hoping for such a move, and they encouraged MacNeill to found the Irish Volunteers. Many of the officers were members of the brotherhood which hoped to use the new movement to organise a rebellion."

From *Ireland Three* by M E Collins, 1972.

SOURCE F

Irish Volunteers parading near Sligo.

?

1 What evidence is there that the Irish Volunteers were active in the North of Ireland? (**A,C** and **D**)

2 Explain why you think Irish Volunteer groups were formed in the North of Ireland. (**T**)

3 Study the pictures. What do they tell you about the organisation and discipline of the Irish Volunteer Force? (**A,D** and **F**)

4 Using the information in this section, construct a time-line showing Redmond's role in the formation and early days of the IVF up to June 1914.

5 The main reason for members of the IRB joining the IVF was that their organisation was almost dead and they were looking for new life. Say why you agree or disagree with this statement.

3.8 Gun-Running in the North

SOURCE A

Members of the UVF loading their guns at Craigavon during
the Curragh emergency, March 1914.

SOURCE B

A contemporary postcard.

SOURCE C

THE PRINCIPAL MEMBERS OF THE PROVISIONAL GOVERNMENT
OF ULSTER, 1914. Can you see Carson and Craig?

SOURCE D

"Sir Hubert Gough, commander of the
Cavalry Brigade at the Curragh, notified
Paget that he and fifty-nine of his other
officers chose ... the alternative of
dismissal from the service."

From *The Bold Fenian Men* by
Robert Kee, 1972.

SOURCE E

"Under the mistaken impression that they
were about to be ordered to take action
against the Ulster Unionists, fifty eight
officers of the 3rd Cavalry Regiment
stationed at the Curragh, ... said that
they would rather be dismissed than
move against the North."

From *A History of Northern Ireland*
by Patrick Buckland, 1981.

If Asquith and his colleagues had not been immediately
alarmed by the formation of the UVF in January 1913, the presence of two
private armies in Ireland at the beginning of 1914 was certainly a cause
for concern. Throughout 1913 Unionists in the North had been involved in
several attempts to smuggle small quantities of arms into the province for
use by the UVF. Even the King was alarmed by this, and he asked
Asquith if it was his intention to use the British Army to bring the UVF
under control. In fact, Asquith had already considered the difficulty of
using the army in Ulster. He knew that while the British Army was
supposed to be detached from politics, the officer class supported the
Conservative party, and many were known to be sympathetic to the Ulster
cause. The problem reached a climax in March 1914.

3.8

THE CURRAGH INCIDENT
MARCH 1914

Knowing that the UVF was desperate for arms, the War Office issued orders to the army stationed in Ireland to take the necessary precautions to improve security at barracks and arms depots in Ulster. The stores at Enniskillen, Omagh and Armagh were all considered to be at risk from a UVF attack. The main army base in Ireland was at the Curragh in Co. Kildare, and it was here that a very strange incident, known as the **Curragh incident**, began. A considerable number of officers at the Curragh thought that they were going to be sent to Ulster, where they believed, probably mistakenly, that they would be ordered to attack the UVF. In the confusion one general, **Sir Hubert Gough**, informed the Commander-in-Chief that he and more that 50 other officers would resign if they were ordered to move against Ulster. Panic followed. The War Office hastily produced a scheme to allow any officer who had lived in Ulster to opt out of any such action, but this failed to satisfy the officers at the Curragh. By the time Asquith got to hear about the crisis at the Curragh, the government was facing a potential army mutiny at a time when international tension was rising as war approached. Taking the cautious line, Asquith indicated that the British Army would not be used to force Home Rule on Ulster. He had little choice, because it was doubtful if the army could be relied upon to take the necessary action. Carson and the Unionists were now in a very strong position.

THE UVF AND THE
CURRAGH CRISIS

Back in September 1911, Ulster Unionists had indicated their intention to form a **Provisional Government** for the province if Home Rule ever became law. Two years later detailed plans for such a scheme were formulated by Carson and Craig. The personnel involved were all informed of their responsibilities, and arrangements were made for replacements if the Ulster leaders were arrested. During the Curragh crisis, when it appeared that the Asquith government would order the arrest of the Unionist leadership, the members of the Ulster provisional government assembled at Craigavon, Craig's Co. Down home, where they were guarded by a detachment of armed Ulster Volunteers.

SOURCE **F**

SAVIOURS OF ULSTER.
(THE IMMORTAL ONE HUNDRED,)

One Hundred Noble Officers, of England's pride to-day,
Have stood upon the Curragh Camp a summons to obey,
Their General said "I've orders that to Ulster you must go,
And there shoot down their loyal men, as you would a foreign foe.
The Government of England, in the hands of roguish knaves,
Give orders, spite of conscience, you must this Home Rule save,
For we're pledged to John Redmond them to Roman bondage drag,
Their only crime, we must confess, is loyalty to the flag."

CHORUS—
But it is a famous story, proclaim it far and near,
Of this noble band, *One Hundred*, who stood for honour dear,
And refused to go to Ulster, their rights to take away,
Or be a party to this plan to give John Redmond sway.

General Paget gave the order ; cried Gough "Can it be true ?
Are we to shoot down loyal men ? why this we cannot do.
We remember, Sir, when England stood in danger grave,
These very men have shed their blood our noble flag to save.
You may order us to Russia, or to the mouth of hell,
But we'll never go to Ulster and enslave those loyal men.
We're loyal, Sir, to England, until the end of time,
But before we'll coerce Ulster our commands we will resign."

Song composed to celebrate the officers of the Curragh camp.

1   What evidence is there that the Ulster Unionists were prepared to take the law into their own hands? (**A**,**C** and **T**)

2   What message is the army officer giving to Redmond in Source **B**?

3   Read carefully the verses in Source **F**. What is the main reason given in this source for the army refusing to go to Ulster?

4   Sources **D**,**E** and **F** all give the number of men who "mutinied" at the Curragh. What are these numbers and why do they differ?

5   Does the fact that these numbers differ mean that none of the sources is reliable? Explain your answer.

3.8 Gun-Running in the North (continued)

THE LARNE GUN-RUNNING

The UVFs position was further strengthened by the arrival of a large shipment of arms in the province the following month. In January 1914 Carson and Craig had approved an ambitious project by the fanatical Ulster Unionist, Fred Crawford, to purchase a huge consignment of arms in Germany, and bring them to Ulster in a ship which he had bought in Glasgow for £4,500. On the night of the 24/25 April 1914 the ship, the **Clyde Valley**, delivered its cargo. Small numbers of weapons were put ashore at **Bangor** and **Donaghadee**, but the main shipment was brought to **Larne** in Co. Antrim. The scene in Larne that April night was remarkable. The UVF had cordoned off the town, and the force's **Motor Car Corps** quickly delivered the rifles to centres all over the province. In total nearly 25,000 rifles and three million rounds of ammunition had arrived. One notable feature of the Larne gun-running was the absence of any police attempt to prevent the dispatch of the arms shipment once it had been landed. To Nationalists it appeared that the local police chiefs had not interfered with the UVF, because they were sympathetic to their aims.

SOURCE G

THE ARMING OF ULSTER

Gigantic Coup Effected

HUGE GUN-RUNNING SCHEME

Many Thousands of Rifles Landed

Headlines in the *Belfast News-Letter* 27 April 1914.

SOURCE H

BRAVO, ULSTER! UNLOADING THE GUNS AT BANGOR PIER.

'Arrangements were made to 'short circuit' (not to cut or damage) all telegraph and 'phone wires to Larne at Magheramorne, at 9.15 pm after last train had gone down ...

GPO Exchange was watched carefully - all operators being special men - also night telegraph staff! ...

At 11pm a vessel came dead slow up the channel and took about 25 minutes to get alongside. By this time 15 customs officers ... had collected. As the vessel came alongside the customs hailed her, 'What's your cargo?' Skipper replied. 'I am instructed to tell you it's coal.'

... I returned to head quarters 4.30 am, found reports all correct from Larne ...

At Bangor all worked well, ditto at Donaghadee, although they did not start to unload there 'till 6 am and finished at 8 am!'

SOURCE I

Extracts from Capt. F Hall's description of the gun-running, including the diversion staged in Belfast that night.

SOURCE **J**

SEARCHING FOR ARMS IN ULSTER.

AN ULSTER VOLUNTEER : "Sure don't ye see
    I've got no **arms**, constable?"
CONSTABLE : "They must be hid in the **Ulster**,
    then."
(About 100,000 rifles and machine guns are
hidden in Ulster. An **Ulster** was a nickname for
a particular style of overcoat,)

SOURCE **K**

BRAVO, ULSTER VOLUNTEERS!   The Gun Runners on the road to Belfast from Larne.

Sources H, J, K and L
were postcards issued in
1914 to celebrate the
Larne Gun-running,
which was regarded as a
major propaganda coup.

SOURCE **L**

SEEK AND YE SHALL FIND!

Historic Events Series]   SEARCHING FOR ARMS IN ULSTER.   [No. 8

?

1   What can we learn from Sources
H,I and **K** about the degree of
organisation by the UVF for the
gun-running?

2   The Belfast Newsletter was widely
regarded as a Unionist paper.
How does this affect the reliability
of its headlines? (**G**)

3   How do Sources **J** and **L** portray
the police search for arms in
Ulster?

4   Sources **J** and **L** are cartoons. As
such can they be regarded as
reliable evidence? Explain your
answer.

3.9 Gun-Running in the South

SOURCE A

On board the *Asgard*. From left to right: Mrs. Childers, Miss Mary Spring-Rice, Cptn. Gordon Shephard, Pat McGinley

SOURCE B

"I was on the head of the East Pier [at Howth] about noon when I noticed a white-painted yawl of at least 50 tons, smartly kept and steered by a lady ... She had on board an unusual number of men, many of whom were obviously not professional sailors ...

Turning round at that moment I saw at least a couple of hundred men running for all they were worth towards the pier from the direction of the railway station, while three or four hundred ran to the head of the pier ... Some of the men were in uniform, some had only badges, but all of them carried long oak life-preservers, and their officers carried revolvers in their hands. The majority of the men seemed to have come from Dublin. While they were running up the pier, the hatches of the yawl were opened. Some of the men from the pier jumped down and handed up to their comrades Lee-Enfield rifles of recent pattern, wrapped in straw ... a large number of rifles and boxes of ammunition were taken away in taxicabs and private motor cars. A small machine gun, with wheels, was also taken off the yawl ... It was evident that every man knew exactly what they had to do ... A very remarkable feature was that the whole affair was conducted almost in silence, very few orders being given."

Unloading the rifles: An eye-witness's story. *The Irish Times*, 27 July 1914.

SOURCE C

"The rifles were landed at Howth and the Nationalist Volunteers proceeded to march with them to Dublin. They were intercepted by police and troops at Clontarf, and as they resisted attempts to disarm them, the soldiers made a bayonet charge, dispersing the Volunteers, several of whom were wounded. The others made off, taking most of the rifles with them.

It was in Dublin ... that the most serious incident occurred. As the troops were returning, a Nationalist mob gathered and stoned them along the road. The order was then given to fire, and as the result of a volley, many were wounded, four being killed or dying later in hospital."

Belfast News-Letter, 27 July 1914.

The Irish Volunteers intended to match the UVF in their gun-running exploits. A number of senior figures in the Volunteers, including several IRB men, were busily engaged in arranging the purchase of arms for the movement. Like the UVF, the Irish Volunteers bought weapons in Germany and then transported them to Ireland on board a yacht owned by the dedicated Home Ruler, **Erskine Childers**. The yacht, the **Asgard**, arrived at **Howth**, Co. Dublin, on **26 July 1914**. A total of 1,500 rifles and 45,000 rounds of ammunition were landed at Howth harbour and then quickly dispatched by the Volunteers. In this instance the police had tried to intervene to prevent the distribution of the weapons, but in the confusion which followed the Volunteers managed to ship the rifles away. In fact, many of them were sent to Dublin in taxis which had been organised to assemble close to the harbour.

THE BACHELOR'S WALK SHOOTING

The scene that Sunday afternoon was one of confusion. In their attempt to seize the arms the police had asked for assistance, and a number of troops from the King's Own Scottish Borderers had marched out to reinforce the police. When it was clear that it would be impossible to disarm the Volunteers, the soldiers were ordered to march the three miles back to Dublin, but on their journey they were followed by a small, hostile crowd which was jeering at the troops' failure to disarm the Volunteers. By the time they had reached **Bachelor's Walk**, a quay on the River Liffey, the soldiers lost their discipline, when stones and bottles were thrown, and they fired into the crowd. Three people were killed and a further thirty-eight were wounded.

The Irish reacted bitterly to this incident. After all, the police and army had stood by three months earlier, when a much larger shipment of arms had arrived in Larne. It was obvious that the authorities were treating the Irish Volunteers very differently to the UVF, and this provided the more extreme Nationalists, particularly the IRB, with a useful propaganda advantage. The result of the Howth gun-running was that two armed camps were now present in Ireland - one determined to have Home Rule, the other equally determined to prevent it. Civil war was very much on the cards.

SOURCE E

"Mr. John Redmond asked the Chief Secretary in the House of Commons yesterday to give information about the gun-running and rioting in Dublin and Mr. Birrell [Chief Secretary] ... stated that the Assistant Commissioner of the Dublin Metropolitan Police acted on his own responsibility in requisitioning the military, and that he had been suspended pending an inquiry. He added that the soldiers fired on the mob in Dublin without orders ... Mr. Birrell defended the inaction of the Government in regard to the Ulster Volunteers, and said there should be similar inaction in the case of the Nationalist Volunteers."

Belfast News-Letter 28 July 1914.

SOURCE D

"Last evening a deplorable affair occurred on Bachelor's Walk, near the foot of Liffey Street. A force of King's Own Scottish Borderers marching back to barracks after intercepting National Volunteers who had been gun-running at Howth, were assailed by a mob, and retaliated by firing on the people. Three lives were lost, and between twenty and thirty persons injured."

The Irish Times, 27 July 1914.

1 What are the strengths and weaknesses of using only the eye witness account of the gun-running at Howth? (**B**)

2 In what ways do Sources **C** and **D** agree or disagree about the incident following the gun-running?

3 How might the Irish Chief Secretary's account (Source **E**) have been influenced by the Government's fears of civil violence in Ireland at a moment when war was threatening Europe?

4 Use the information in this section to write two brief accounts of the Bachelor's Walk incident - (a) From the point of view of a soldier in The King's Own Scottish Borderers. (b) From an Irish Volunteer viewpoint.

5 Explain why these accounts would differ.

3.10 The Buckingham Palace Conference

SOURCE A

King George and Queen Mary Opening the New Irish Parliament

A postcard printed in 1914. It was based on a photograph taken during the royal visit in 1911. The scene shown never actually happened.

SOURCE B

'There was no surprise in the lobby when it became known early this afternoon that the Conference had terminated without any agreement being arrived at. The secrets of the conference have been well kept, and yet sufficient was known on the second day of proceedings to justify the most pessimistic view of the issue. It was realised with regret that the representatives of the various parties were all too deeply pledged to their supporters to maintain their separate lines of policy for any accommodation to be possible ...'

The Irish Times 25 July 1914.

SOURCE C

OH! WHAT A FALL THERE'LL BE.

*Carson clinging staunch
To a weak and falling branch,
Thinks he'll saw a way out of Home Rule;
And he'll never, never stop,
'Till he gets an awful drop;
For he works with an impossible tool*

On the political front 1914 was a bad year for the IPP. Ever since the Home Rule crisis began in 1912, Redmond had maintained that Ulster could not be given special treatment, because Ireland was one nation and could never be divided. Redmond's mistake, however, was to depend too much on the Liberal government to resist Unionist claims for the exclusion of Ulster. In February 1914 Asquith had assured the Irish leader that all his cabinet colleagues were opposed to giving Ulster special treatment. This was not true. In the following month Redmond had no other choice but to agree to the government producing proposals which might satisfy the Unionists. What the government proposed was a scheme whereby any Irish county could opt out of a Home Rule parliament for a period of six years. This would be decided by a vote or plebiscite in each county. In reality this meant that the four counties in North-East Ulster with a Protestant majority, **Antrim**, **Down**, **Londonderry**, and **Armagh**, would opt out of Home Rule on a temporary basis. Confident that he now had a clear advantage Carson rejected the proposals out of hand. The Unionist leader had been offered four counties, but he knew that if he stood firm, he could get two more. This was his intention.

The Curragh incident and the gun-running episodes in the North and the South then inflamed an already tense situation. With Home Rule due to become law in 1914 many people in England believed that civil war in Ireland was inevitable, as it appeared that Carson would refuse to back down. This situation greatly alarmed the King who had earlier expressed deep concern over the Home Rule crisis. Desperate to halt the slide into civil war the King urged Asquith to hold talks with the party leaders in a final effort to reach a compromise. The King gave an opening

SOURCE D

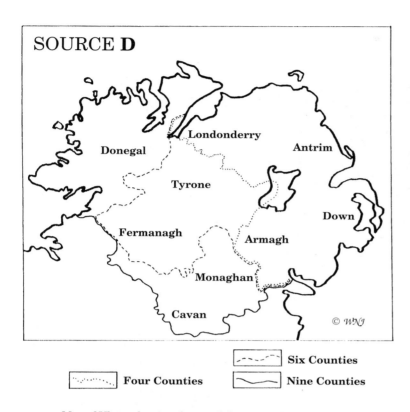

Map of Ulster showing the possibile options for partition.

Legend:
- - - - - - **Six Counties**
.... **Four Counties**
~~~~ **Nine Counties**

SOURCE E

> "*BUCKINGHAM PALACE*
> *The Conference held meetings on the 21st, 22nd, 23rd, and 24th of July respectively. The possibility of defining an area to be excluded from the operation of the Government of Ireland Bill was considered. The Conference being unable to agree either in principle or in detail upon such an area brought its meetings to a conclusion. (signed) JW Lowther   24th July 1914.*"

Press release by Buckingham Palace.

SOURCE F

> "*The Palace conference is now a thing of the past. In a week it has come and it has gone and in a sense the net result is nothing, for it has failed to bring forth a settlement that would avoid civil war... The Prime Minister ... announced that in the circumstances the Government proposed to take the Government of Ireland Amending Bill on an early day next week ... What are we to deduce from this: that the Government has reverted to the ante-Conference position?*"

Belfast News-Letter 24 July 1914.

address to the **Buckingham Palace Conference** on 21 July 1914, and it lasted until 24 July, when negotiations broke down. Nationalists, Unionists, Liberals and Conservatives were all represented at these round table talks, and endless maps and figures were produced. Asquith and Lloyd George were present for the Liberals, Bonar Law and Lord Lansdowne for the Conservatives, Carson and Craig for the Unionists, while Redmond and his deputy, John Dillon, represented the IPP. The talks took place in a friendly atmosphere, but the representatives still could not agree on the area of Ulster territory to be excluded from Home Rule. Back in March, Redmond had reluctantly agreed to the temporary exclusion of Antrim, Down, Londonderry and Armagh, but at the conference Carson also demanded **Tyrone** and **Fermanagh**, and Redmond would not accept this. The Buckingham Palace Conference seemed to present the last opportunity for a settlement. When the talks broke down, the British expected civil war, but a new international event, which made local disputes in Europe appear tiny in comparison, quickly overtook events in Ireland. This was the First World War.

1   Suggest reasons why the Nationalists printed the postcard on page 54. (**A**)

2   Why is the saw in Source **C** described as 'an impossible tool'?

3   Why do you think the King had intervened at this time? (**T**)

4   How does Source **F** indicate that no progress had been made?

5   Would you agree with the view in the Irish Times (Source **B**) that the failure of the conference was no surprise? Explain your answer.

4.1 Ireland and the First World War

SOURCE A

A field service postcard.   Soldiers were given cards like these to write home.

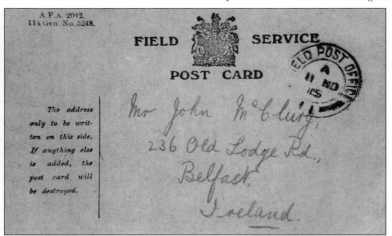

The war with Germany had begun in August 1914, and everyone's attention shifted off the Home Rule subject. Yet the Home Rule Bill was due to become law, and some kind of political decision had to be made. Accordingly, Home Rule became law on 18 September, but with it Asquith also introduced another measure to suspend the operation of Home Rule. The politicians intended to return to the problem at the end of the war. The question of what to do with Ulster had not been solved; it had merely been put on the shelf, where it would stay until a more appropriate opportunity presented itself.

THE ULSTER DIVISION

The War strengthened the position of the Ulster Unionists, but damaged Redmond and the IPP beyond repair. Having spent the past three years loudly proclaiming loyalty to King and Empire, Carson had little alternative but to offer the UVF for armed service in the war. The government welcomed Carson's offer of help. Of course, the members of the UVF had already received military training, and were thus ideal recruiting material. The War Office agreed to Carson's suggestion that a separate division of the British Army should be formed from these UVF recruits, and 10,000 soon joined what became known as the 36th Ulster Division. Already Craig had taken a decision to place an order for new uniforms for the division, which were paid for by wealthy Unionist supporters in Britain. Recruiting meetings and parades were held all over the province, as Craig, Carson and the other Unionist leaders urged Protestants to join up. Their objective in this was clear. The Unionist leaders were convinced that if they helped Britain in her hour of need, the British would not force Home Rule on them, when the war was over. By April 1915 the Unionist newspaper, the Belfast Newsletter, was claiming that 35,000 men from Ulster had joined the British Army.

SOURCE B

"The grave crisis ... has had the effect of accentuating the patriotic spirit of the Ulster Volunteer Force and the steps taken by Sir Edward Carson to inform the Government of the desire of a large number of the members to give their service ... have met with the hearty approval of the rank and file. The organisation has risen to a great occasion with a praiseworthy spontaneity and enthusiasm, bearing out to the full the frequent references of Sir Edward Carson to the loyalty of the force and their readiness to do everything in their power to uphold the noble traditions of the British race..."

Belfast News-Letter, 8 August 1914.

THE IRISH DIVISIONS

In the South Redmond was behaving in an equally patriotic manner, but he did not receive the same treatment as Carson and the Ulstermen. His call for a separate Irish Division was ignored, and the Irish Volunteers who enlisted were scattered throughout British regiments. From the outset Redmond believed that by displaying support for Britain in the war and by encouraging Irish Nationalists to fight for Britain, Ireland would be rewarded at the end of the war. When news of the outbreak of war was announced in the House of Commons, Redmond promised the co-operation of the Volunteers in organising Irish defences against a possible German attack. Six weeks later, however, he went further, when he told a Volunteer parade at Woodenbridge, Co. Wicklow, that they should go to the front line in France to fight for the British Empire. This was a courageous move, but other Nationalists were not certain that it was a wise one. Redmond's Woodenbridge speech split the Volunteers. By September 1914 they numbered 180,000, and while the vast majority still supported Redmond, a significant group of approximately 10,000 men formed a new splinter group under the original leader, Eoin MacNeill. This group retained the name Irish Volunteers, while Redmond's supporters were now referred to as the National Volunteers. Many of these National Volunteers joined the British Army, and by 1915 the Asquith government was describing the response of Irish Nationalists to the war as 'magnificent'.

SINN FEIN AND THE WAR

The pattern of recruitment in the South was similar to Ulster in that most of the recruits came from Irish towns, where there was often high unemployment, and low wages and poor conditions for those in work. Ideally, however, these were not the men wanted by the army. Farmers' sons would have been ideal recruiting material as they were already fit and naturally strong, but this group was very slow in joining up. The main reason for this was that farmers were earning more money in wartime, as the demand for food from Britain rose sharply. Consequently, these farmers' sons, many of whom would have emigrated in the past, could stay on the farm and live a comfortable life. They were also listening to a new political party in Ireland which was making an increasing impact in 1915 by urging Irishmen not to join the British Army. This was Sinn Fein. It stressed that the conflict in Europe was Britain's war, not Ireland's.

Redmond, like most of the political leaders, had assumed in August 1914 that the war would be a short affair, but the longer the war dragged on, the weaker his position became. More extreme groups, such as Sinn Fein, were becoming increasingly critical of the IPP. Although a majority of the people continued to support Redmond, this support was no longer enthusiastic, and it was clear that if a more attractive alternative appeared, the IPP would be in serious difficulty.

SOURCE D

"Is it too much to hope that out of this situation there may spring a result which will be good, not merely for the Empire, but good for the future welfare and integrity of the Irish nation."

From a speech by John Redmond in the House of Commons, 3 August 1914.

SOURCE C

"The duty of the manhood of Ireland is twofold. Its duty is at all costs to defend the shores of Ireland against foreign invasion. It is a duty more than that, of taking care that Irish valour proves itself on the field of war as it has always proved itself in the past ...

I am glad to see such magnificent material for soldiers around me, and I say to you 'Go on drilling and make yourselves efficient for the work, and then account for yourselves as men, not only in Ireland itself, but wherever the firing line extends, in defence of right, of freedom, and of religion in this war.'"

Speech by John Redmond to the Irish Volunteers at Woodenbridge, 20 September 1920.

1 How can you tell from Source **A** that soldiers' mail home was heavily censored?

2 Why should such censorship take place?

3 What reasons are given for:
(a) The Ulster Volunteers   and
(b) The Irish Volunteers being encouraged to join the army in August/September 1914? (**B,C,D** and **T**)

4 Design a recruiting poster encouraging Irish or Ulster men to go to war for Britain.

4.2 The Battle of the Somme

SOURCE A

At Thiepval, 1st July, 1916.

The Charge of the Ulster Division at Thiepval, 1 July 1916. This famous postcard originally appeared as a Christmas card in 1916.

By 1916 the war on the Western Front had reached a position of stalemate. Huge numbers of men were dug into trench systems, and they fought each other across what became known as 'No Man's Land'. When one side attacked, they were easy targets and usually driven back by the enemy. In 1916 the British and French generals were ready to try and break the stalemate in an attempt to secure a decisive advantage in the conflict. Their plan was for a massive infantry attack to follow a sustained period of artillery bombardment. The place chosen was the area along the **River Somme**, and the date was set for the 1 July.

SOURCE B

"It is impossible to think without emotion of the many brave men from our province who have laid down their lives in vindicating their loyalty and devotion to the Empire, but we have the consolation of knowing that they have met with a glorious death ... for the deeds they have accomplished will live in history, and future generations will find in their dauntless courage a great and noble inspiration. They have not died in vain..."

Belfast News-Letter, Friday 7 July 1916.

SOURCE C

'Today many more casualties are reported among the officers and men of the Ulster Division, and the people at home are now realising to the full the enormous sacrifices which were made by [them]... In the course of one short week hundreds of Ulster homes have been plunged into mourning,... whilst they mourn ... their grief is softened by the pride they feel in what has been achieved by the sacrifices.'

Belfast News-Letter, Saturday 8 July 1916.

SOURCE D

"Well may Ulstermen inscribe on their banners the year '1916' beside that of '1688'. For Ulstermen have struck another blow for civil and religious liberty ... but the bereavements will be to some extent mellowed by the knowledge that all have done their duty so nobly and have fallen in the hour of victory with their faces towards the enemy."

Tyrone Constitution, 14 July 1916.

THE ULSTER DIVISION

The Ulster Division had arrived in France in October 1915, and by the summer of 1916 they had been moved to the Somme area, where they were to play a prominent role in the battle. The battle plan, however, was seriously flawed, and the British Army suffered appalling casualties, many from machine-gun fire, on the first day. A total of 60,000 casualties had been recorded, many in the first hour of the attack, and of these 21,000 had died. The Ulster Division, in particular, had sustained heavy casualties. Over 5,000 men were wounded, and of these at least 2,000 died. Despite these terrible losses, the Ulster Division performed with great bravery on that first day. They were the only division to take all their objectives, but they then had to retreat due to the lack of support. Back in Ulster there was naturally great sorrow among the population, as so many families had been affected, but there was also a sense of pride. The first day of the Battle of the Somme saw the heaviest losses ever sustained by the British Army in one day, and the Ulster Division ranked fourth in the table of losses. The Unionist leadership was confident that this supreme sacrifice would be taken into consideration, when the Ulster question came up for discussion after the war.

SOURCE E

Field Marshal Sir Henry Wilson and Lady Wilson visiting the trenches at Thiepval where the Ulster Division soldiers fell. Sir Henry Wilson had been closely associated with the UVF.

SOURCE F

"On Saturday 1 July the north of Ireland had gone about its business, oblivious of the battle raging in France. On Monday morning the Belfast Newsletter reported that 'The long-awaited Franco-British offensive' had begun. Then on Thursday 6 the paper published Maj. General Nugent's special order to the 36th Division delivered before the battle."

From *The Road to the Somme*
by Philip Orr, 1987.

SOURCE G

"I can think of nothing but what might have been - and of the golden friends I had ... hence my fury at how they were almost obliterated through gross stupidity."

Malcolm McKee (a Somme veteran), speaking in 1966.

?

1 How many years are there between the writing of Source **G** and Sources **B,C** and **D**?

2 How do the views on the Battle of the Somme expressed in Source **G** differ from the views expressed in Sources **B**, **C** and **D**?

3 Give reasons why these views differ.

4 Most of these written sources come from pro-Unionist newspapers. How does this affect their reliability?

4.3 The Easter Rising

Although Nationalists had fought with equal valour in the British Army, a growing number of Irishmen were beginning to question the wisdom of Redmond's total support for Britain. The split in the Volunteers in September 1914 had given clear expression to this development. Eoin MacNeill's breakaway group of Irish Volunteers continued to drill and practise weapons training. Their intention was to have a trained force ready to insist on Home Rule at the end of the war. This situation, however, played into the hands of the small band of violent Nationalists, the IRB. MacNeill's group with just over 10,000 members was the ideal size for the IRB to infiltrate and seek to influence. The IRB also saw an opportunity, while Britain was engaged in a desperate struggle for survival in the war with Germany. An old Fenian idea had been, 'England's difficulty is Ireland's opportunity', and the IRB did not want to miss the opportunity of striking a blow for Irish freedom, while Britain was caught up in the war. Consequently, a Military Council of the IRB was created in 1915 to plan a rebellion.

PLANNING THE RISING

Previous attempts to overthrow British rule in Ireland had failed, in part because government spies always seemed to know what the extreme Nationalists had planned. In 1915, therefore, secrecy was to be the key in the planning of a rising. The main figures in the IRB plot were **Patrick Pearse** and **Tom Clarke**, and the Military Council proceeded to make the arrangements without informing the Irish Volunteers, who were to be involved, or even the rest of the IRB leadership. In January 1916 the plotters were joined by **James Connolly** and his 200 strong **Irish Citizen Army (ICA)**, which had been formed during a labour dispute towards the end of 1913. Connolly was a socialist, and he hoped that a successful rising would move Ireland closer to socialism.

The date of the rising was fixed for Easter 1916, and **Roger Casement** had organised a shipment of arms, for use by the Irish Volunteers, to arrive from Germany. However, the German ship carrying the arms was intercepted by the Royal Navy, and the 20,000 rifles destined for Ireland were lost. Casement was also captured shortly after he came ashore. This caused the Military Council to postpone the rising for twenty-four hours until Easter Monday, but without the weapons from Germany the Easter Rising was doomed to fail. Yet Pearse and the other members of the Military Council, which now numbered seven, were determined to go ahead. They believed that a rising would result in their making a sacrifice in blood which would stir the Irish people into supporting a more extreme

SOURCE A

"For England may keep faith
For all that is done and said.
We knew their dream; enough
To know they dreamed and are dead;
And what if excess of love
Bewildered them till they died?
I write it out in a verse -
MacDonagh and MacBride
And Connolly and Pearse
Now and in time to be,
Wherever green is worn,
Are changed, changed utterly;
A terrible beauty is born."

From *Easter 1916*, by W B Yeats.

SOURCE B

Irish Rebellion - May 1916.
Soldiers holding a Dublin Street.

British soldiers pose behind a barricade in a Dublin street.

SOURCE C

"We declare the right of the people of Ireland to the ownership of Ireland..."

"We hereby proclaim the Irish Republic..."

"The Irish Republic is entitled to the allegiance of every Irishman and Irishwoman."

Extracts from the *Proclamation of the Irish Republic*, (read by Pearse from the front of the GPO, Easter 1916).

form of Nationalism than the brand on offer from Redmond and the IPP.

EASTER WEEK 1916

On Easter Monday morning, the **24 April 1916**, about 1500 Volunteers and ICA took to the streets, and occupied a number of important buildings in the centre of Dublin. The most significant of these was the **General Post Office (GPO)** in what is now O'Connell Street. From the front of the GPO, Pearse read out the **Proclamation of the Irish Republic**, which had been signed by the seven members of the IRB's Military Council. The signatories were Patrick Pearse, Tom Clarke, James Connolly, Sean MacDermott, Joseph Plunkett, Eamonn Ceannt and Thomas MacDonagh, and they proclaimed an Irish Republic free from British Rule. However, the reaction of the people of Dublin to the Easter rebels was extremely hostile. A good part of the city had been destroyed in the fighting between the rebels and the British troops, and after six days of hostilities Pearse and his followers were forced to surrender. As they were marched away after their arrest, they were jeered by a large number of the city's residents. During the rebellion approximately 450 people had been killed, and there was considerable damage to property.

THE AFTERMATH OF THE RISING

The British response to the Easter Rising was swift and harsh. Nearly 3500 people were imprisoned, many more than had taken part in the rising, and from 3 to 12 May fifteen executions were carried out. All seven signatories of the Proclamation were executed, including James Connolly who had been so seriously wounded during the fighting that he had to be tied to a chair. Casement was later hanged in London after being found guilty of treason. These killings shocked the Irish people and soon created a great wave of sympathy for the Easter rebels. The British made another blunder after the rising, when they announced that the rebellion was the work of Sinn Fein, rather than the IRB. At the time Sinn Fein was the best known of the more extreme Nationalist groups, and was therefore blamed for the rising. When people began to turn away from Redmond and the IPP, who were now criticised for assisting the British war effort, they looked to Sinn Fein for leadership.

SOURCE D

> *'We seem to have lost, we have not lost. To refuse to fight would have been to lose... We have kept faith with the past and handed a tradition to the future...'*

Patrick Pearse, speaking at his court martial in May 1916.

SOURCE E

The Quays from O'Connell's Bridge, Dublin (After the Rebellion)

O'Connell Bridge showing people looking at the damage to the centre of Dublin, taken the day after the Rising ended.

?

1 Source **A** is written by Yeats who was part of the Gaelic Revival movement - therefore it must be unreliable. Explain why you agree or disagree with this statement.

2 Who is likely to have taken the picture (Source **B**) opposite, and why was it taken?

3 What factors may have influenced Pearse when writing the 'Proclamation of the Irish Republic', and making a speech at his court martial? (**C** and **D**).

4 How can you tell from Source **E** that the flames were added after the photograph was taken?

5 What other types of evidence would you require to write a full account of the Easter Rising?

4.4 The Rise of Sinn Fein

SOURCE A

Sinn Fein, meaning 'Ourselves', was led by Arthur Griffith, a Dublin journalist who had founded the party in 1905. Griffith's exact political aims were complicated, but it was clear that Sinn Fein wanted much more freedom for Ireland than Home Rule would confer. Yet the party had attracted little public attention until 1916. What Sinn Fein did have, however, was a romantic name and an association with the heroes of Easter week, because of Britain's error in dubbing the Easter Rising a Sinn Fein rebellion, even though Sinn Fein had not taken part in the rising. With Redmond and the IPP now out of favour, many Irishmen were looking for a new energetic party which could challenge British rule in Ireland. It appeared that a modified version of the old Sinn Fein party might supply this need.

A propaganda postcard.

BY - ELECTION VICTORIES 1917

The Sinn Fein movement which emerged in 1917 was a mixture of different elements. It contained the old Sinn Fein party, the Volunteers, some senior IRB figures and many disgruntled former IPP supporters. Sinn Fein was soon given an opportunity to test its strength in a series of by-elections which were called in 1917. In the first of these, in February 1917 **Count George Plunkett**, the father of Joseph Plunkett, one of the executed leaders of the 1916 rising, won a comfortable victory after a campaign in which recently released Irish Volunteers had played an enthusiastic role. In May, July and August three more Sinn Fein candidates won seats from the IPP, with the most significant being the election of **Eamon de Valera** for East Clare in July 1917.

De Valera was the senior surviving figure from the Easter Rising, and had been sentenced to death by the British for his part in the rebellion. His execution, however, was not carried out, and he was released from prison, along with the other senior prisoners from Easter week, in June 1917. In the East Clare by-election de Valera made it absolutely clear that he was demanding full independence for a new Irish Republic which would enjoy complete freedom from Britain. The Irish Volunteers again featured prominently in his campaign, and a new election slogan, 'Up the Republic!', was widely used, though precisely what methods would be employed to achieve this republic were never clarified by de Valera. Yet despite his victory, neither de Valera nor the other three new Sinn Fein MPs, took their seats in the Westminster parliament. This policy was known as **abstention**, an old idea of Griffith's, and it proved popular with Irish voters.

SOURCE B

'The execution of sixteen of the insurgents over a period of ten days, combined with the arrest of 3400 Sinn Fein activists and sympathisers throughout the country caused many to change their minds. Resentment at the rebels' conduct was overshadowed by resentment at their fate ...'

'...by late 1917 they (Sinn Fein) were acknowledged almost everywhere as the leaders and representatives of the great bulk of Irish opinion ...'

'...the winning of widespread public support had been achieved for it, long before it began to engage in electioneering and propaganda work; the British Government's reaction to the Rising had seen to that.'

From: *The Unification of Sinn Fein in 1917,* by Michael Laffin.

4.4

?

1 What does Source **A** say about Sinn Fein's view of the British Government's attempts to solve the Irish people's problems?

2 What reasons are given in Source **B** to explain the rise in support for Sinn Fein?

3 Why did the hunger strikes take place? (**C** and **T**)

4 What effect did the death of Thomas Ashe have on Sinn Fein propaganda? (**D** and **T**)

SOURCE C

Relatives of prisoners outside Mountjoy Jail during the hunger strike. Note the picture of the Madonna and Child on the gate.

SOURCE D
The funeral of Thomas Ashe in 1917.

HUNGER STRIKES

By the end of 1917 Sinn Fein was clearly the main force in Irish politics. A total of 1200 Sinn Fein clubs sprang up with a membership approaching 250,000. In October an effort had been made to give firm leadership and clear direction to Sinn Fein at the party's convention. De Valera was elected to two positions, becoming President of Sinn Fein and President of the Volunteers. The aim was to unite the whole Sinn Fein movement so that it could offer even more effective opposition to the British. In the previous month Sinn Fein gained more sympathy, when a senior Volunteer officer, **Thomas Ashe**, died on hunger-strike in Mountjoy Jail on 25 September 1917. Like Pearse and the other heroes of Easter week, Ashe had provided Sinn Fein with a new martyr, and his funeral in Dublin, which was attended by a crowd of nearly 40,000, gave the party a great propaganda boost.

THE IRISH CONVENTION

Throughout 1917 the British government had been worried by Sinn Fein's rise to prominence, but ministers were too pre-occupied with the war to spend the necessary time trying to reach a political settlement in Ireland. **Lloyd George**, who had replaced Asquith as Prime Minister in December 1916, had called an **Irish Convention** in **July 1917**. The idea behind this move was that Irish representatives themselves would meet in an effort to solve the problem, but with Sinn Fein refusing to participate, the Irish Convention was unlikely to produce a solution. Earlier, Lloyd George had been given the task of finding a solution, based on Home Rule, immediately after the Easter Rising. On this occasion he had met separately with Carson and Redmond, and while no settlement was reached, Redmond was further discredited in the eyes of Irish voters, as it appeared that he was the only leader prepared to make concessions. To many Irishmen this was an indication of weakness, and it contributed to the IPP's eventual downfall.

4.5 The 1918 General Election

SOURCE A

Satirical postcard *"The first Irish Conscript."*

Sinn Fein had to wait until the general election of 1918 before it could fully demonstrate its supremacy over the IPP. Victory was assured following an extraordinary sequence of events in April 1918. In March the Germans had launched a great offensive on the Western Front in a final attempt to secure a breakthrough. Although it failed, British resources were stretched to the limit, and the government found itself desperately short of manpower. Back in January 1916 the government had been forced to introduce compulsory military service, or **conscription** as it was called, because the system of voluntary recruitment was not providing enough men. The scheme had not been applied to Ireland, but in the desperation for more men in April 1918 the government took the controversial decision of pushing a new Conscription Bill through parliament to extend conscription to Ireland. There was uproar in the country. Two days later on 18 April 1918 leading figures in Sinn Fein and the IPP met along with the Catholic bishops at the **Mansion House**, Dublin to condemn conscription and organise a campaign to oppose it.

The decision to extend conscription to Ireland was a serious error of judgment on the part of the British government, because every shade of Nationalist opinion regarded conscription as yet another example of British aggression on Ireland. For a time, therefore, all Irish Nationalists were united. Yet while the IPP was as much opposed to conscription as Sinn Fein, in the minds of Irishmen it would be Sinn Fein, led by de Valera, which would provide the more effective opposition. After all, Sinn Fein had been critical of even voluntary recruitment since 1914, whereas the IPP, and Redmond in particular, had earlier been closely identified with the war effort.

SOURCE B

"Sinn Fein aims at securing the establishment of that Republic ... by making use of any and every means available to render impotent the power of England to hold Ireland in subjection by military force or otherwise."

Extracts from the Sinn Fein election manifesto, 1918.

SOURCE C

"Sinn Fein was also much favoured in the election by the greatly enlarged new register which almost trebled the previous Irish electorate ... Another telling factor was that in the course of the election campaign itself Sinn Fein was already revealed as the winning party."

From *Ourselves Alone* by Robert Kee, 1972.

The government was shocked by the level of support for the anti-conscription campaign, and following advice from the army, which thought that a huge number of troops would be required to enforce conscription, it was decided to drop the measure in the short term. Yet conscription was not abandoned altogether, because the British retained their powers to implement conscription without a further debate in parliament. This threat of conscription, always in the background, ensured continued support for Sinn Fein which, right to the end of the war, constantly warned the people to be on their guard against a fresh attempt to impose the measure.

THE 'GERMAN PLOT'

The British made another blunder in May 1918, when almost all the Sinn Fein and Volunteer leaders were arrested. It was alleged that Sinn Fein was involved in a **'German Plot'** to obtain help from Germany for another rising. It is almost certain that no such plot existed and that the British were simply looking for an opportunity to smash Sinn Fein. However, the arrests backfired. Some of the Sinn Fein leaders, including de Valera and Griffith, had prior knowledge of the intended arrests, and they allowed themselves to be taken prisoner in order to win further sympathy and support for their cause.

THE 1918 ELECTION

When a general election was announced at the end of the war, it was clear that Sinn Fein had caught the mood of the country. Under new electoral rules the vote in this general election was given to all men over 21 and all women over 30. This meant that there were almost two million voters in Ireland, the great majority of whom had never voted before. These new electors found the youthful, energetic Sinn Fein party more attractive than the old, tired IPP, which was now led by John Dillon following Redmond's death in March 1918. Dillon's task was hopeless, and in 25 constituencies his party could not even field a candidate to oppose Sinn Fein.

The result of the general election of December 1918 was a landslide victory for Sinn Fein in Ireland. They won 73 seats, while the Unionists won 26. The IPP was victorious in only 6 seats, 5 of which were in Ulster, where they remained a force. As they had stated in their election manifesto, the Sinn Fein MPs intended to abstain from Westminster and form their own legislative assembly in Dublin. It was to be called **Dail Eireann**, and its first meeting was scheduled for **21 January 1919**.

SOURCE D

Harry Boland, Michael Collins and Eamonn De Valera.

SOURCE E

"No-one who has not been in Ireland during the past six weeks can possibly realise how passionate is the resentment which has been aroused .. If they [ie the Roman Catholic bishops and the Parliamentary Party] had not intervened to regularise and moderate popular action, there might well have been bloodshed ... all up and down the country."

Hugh Law (a moderate Home Rule MP for a Co. Donegal constituency) writing in June 1918.

?

1 How can we tell from Source **A** that some people in Ireland were unhappy about being asked to fight in the war?

2 What are the strengths and weaknesses of using only Sinn Fein's election manifesto to explain its success in the 1918 election? **(B)**

3 Source **E** was written by a moderate Nationalist. What effect would his views have had?

4 Write a newspaper article, dated December 1918 explaining why Sinn Fein was so successful.

4.6 The Anglo - Irish War

During the election campaign Sinn Fein had made it clear that they would appeal to the forthcoming Peace Conference which was going to look at the status of other small European nations. This policy had proved popular with the voters, but when Sinn Fein delegates travelled to the Peace Conference in Paris to present their case, they found that Ireland's claim for independence was ignored by American and European statesmen, who even refused to admit the Irish delegation to the conference table.

SOLOHEADBEG

During the period from the election to the meeting of the Dail in late January something of a vacuum existed in Ireland, as it was by no means clear what alternative strategy Sinn Fein would adopt if their claims were rejected at the Peace Conference. It was in these circumstances that the initiative was seized by the Irish Volunteers. On the 21 January 1919, the same day as the first meeting of Dail Eireann, a small band of Volunteers ambushed two policemen escorting a delivery of dynamite to a quarry at **Soloheadbeg**, Co Tipperary. The two Royal Irish Constabulary (RIC) men were shot dead, and this marked the opening of what became known as the **Anglo-Irish War** or **War of Independence**. Altogether in 1919 a total of fourteen policemen and soldiers were killed in similar attacks. At first the public was outraged by the attacks on the RIC men, because they were usually Catholics who were well known in the local area. Indeed, the Catholic church was very critical of these Volunteer operations, and at the beginning a clear distinction was drawn between Sinn Fein and this small number of Volunteers engaged in violence.

THE BRITISH RESPONSE

However, the British response to these incidents soon changed opinions in Ireland about the operations of the Volunteers. They began as isolated attacks, but by 1920 a guerrilla war campaign was under way in various parts of the country. By the autumn of 1920 the Volunteers, now referred to as the **Irish Republican Army** (IRA), had organised themselves into small groups of twenty to thirty men, whose main tactic was laying ambushes for police and troops. These groups were known as **flying columns**. The British never regarded events in Ireland as a 'war', and there was some justification for this. The IRA attacks were small-scale and were confined to limited areas, particularly Dublin city, South Tipperary and West Cork. Yet the number of these attacks was increasing during 1920, and the RIC was forced to abandon barracks in

SOURCE A

Black and Tans on guard duty in Dublin, 1920.

SOURCE B

"Dublin yesterday was the scene of an unprecedented outbreak of organised crime, resulting in the murders of twelve Army officers and ex-officers associated with the bringing to justice of Sinn Fein gunmen. In addition two members of the auxiliary police were shot dead."

Belfast News-Letter, 22 November 1920.

SOURCE C

"Regarding the [morning murders] in which fourteen lives were lost and five persons were wounded; it seemed to be generally agreed that the terrible series of murders was the outcome of a deliberately conceived plan, systematically and ruthlessly carried out."

The Irish Times, 22 November 1920.

some areas. In facing this situation the Lloyd George government considered two alternatives. It could either deploy troops in very large numbers, or it could reinforce the police. The latter option was chosen, mainly because Lloyd George himself refused to believe that a small war was going on in Ireland. Instead he described the IRA as a **murder gang** guilty of committing outrages and intimidating the local population.

THE BLACK AND TANS

Ex-soldiers were signed up in Britain and sent across to reinforce the RIC. As they wore a mixture of army and police uniforms, they were immediately nicknamed the **Black and Tans**. They arrived in March 1920, and further reinforcements were recruited, mostly among ex junior officers, and sent to Ireland in August 1920. They were called the **Auxiliaries**. Both the Auxiliaries and Black and Tans were poorly disciplined, and they resorted to ruthless tactics in the struggle against the IRA. If they were ambushed, they often burned nearby houses in retaliation. These actions were known as **reprisals**, and they quickly turned the people against the Crown Forces, while increasing support for the IRA.

MICHAEL COLLINS

De Valera had left for the United States in June 1919 to campaign for Irish freedom, and during his eighteen month absence the whole Sinn Fein political and military movement was dominated by a new figure, **Michael Collins**. A native of Co. Cork, Collins was the key thinker in the IRA campaign, and despite strenuous efforts by the authorities to arrest him, he evaded capture. This turned him into a romantic hero in the eyes of many Irishmen. One of his successes was his intelligence network which kept him informed of British intentions. In Dublin he formed a group of dedicated IRB men, known as **the Squad**, who carried out assassinations on Collins' instructions. The Squad was responsible for killing eleven suspected British agents on Sunday 21 November 1920, and that afternoon a group of Auxiliaries arrived at a Gaelic football match in Croke Park, Dublin, and fired into the crowd, killing 12 people and wounding a further 60. The day was called **Bloody Sunday**. Before the end of the month an IRA flying column led by **Tom Barry**, one of the most famous local commanders, ambushed a group of 18 Auxiliaries at **Kilmichael**, Co. Cork, killing 17 of them.

THE TRUCE JULY 1921

The scale of the violence was now such that the British had to re-consider their strategy in Ireland. The policy of deploying the Black and Tans and Auxiliaries to reinforce the police had obviously been counter-productive, because their behaviour had turned the entire population against the Crown Forces and ensured a propaganda victory for the IRA. Yet in considering their position in the summer of 1921 it had become clear to Collins and some other IRA leaders that they could never succeed in actually driving the British out of Ireland. An increase in the violence in May and June 1921 brought both sides to realise that the war would have to come to an end. Accordingly, a truce was signed between Sinn Fein and the British government on 11 July 1921. The Anglo-Irish War was now over.

SOURCE D

"Dublin has undergone many ordeals in the past ten years ... but it has seldom enjoyed a greater feeling of relief than that experienced at noon yesterday, when a general truce was observed ... The effect on Dublin citizens was almost magical."

The Irish Times, 12 July 1921.

SOURCE E

"At the Belfast demonstration the chief speaker was Sir James Craig ... Prime Minister of Northern Ireland, who justified the decision of the Government to meet the representatives of Sinn Fein in conference in London, in response to the invitation from Mr. Lloyd George. He said if they had declined to take part in a conference Ulster would have been misrepresented, and a bad impression might have been created. He added that Ulster had nothing to give away, and he would not allow her rights to be tampered with."

Belfast News-Letter, 13 July 1921.

?

1 Photographs and newspapers only provide evidence of one moment in time. This means they are of limited value to the historian. Using the sources in this section explain why you agree or disagree with this statement.

4.7 The Troubles

SOURCE A   Train near Newry wrecked by the IRA in June 1921. It is believed to be conveying back to England the horses used by King George V for the opening of the N Ireland Parliament.

The development of the Anglo-Irish War in the South had serious consequences for Ulster. In July 1920 sectarian strife again erupted in the province. Trouble was sparked by the killing of an Ulsterman, who was serving as a senior police officer in Cork, and the subsequent refusal of train workers to bring his body home for burial by rail. Angry Protestants in the shipyard then retaliated by expelling Catholic workmen, and the usual pattern of violence followed. These clashes in the summer marked the beginning of **The Troubles**, which lasted until June 1922 and claimed over 2,000 victims with 428 of these being killed. This time, however, the violence spread outside Belfast to medium-sized towns such as Lisburn and Banbridge. IRA units in the North attacked the Crown Forces, and this provoked a predictable response. As the level of violence mounted, Unionists demanded the formation of a new body to assist the army and police in Ulster. Craig, who was now serving as a junior minister in the British government, put forward detailed proposals for a new force of special constables who would help to restore order in the various trouble spots in the North.. Fearing the re-appearance of the UVF if it delayed, the government agreed to Craig's scheme, and permission was granted for the formation of the **Ulster Special Constabulary** in September 1920.

THE B SPECIALS AND THE IRA

The **Specials** were an exclusively Protestant force, and some of its part-time members, who were known as **B Specials** as opposed to the full time A Specials, were suspected of taking part in attacks on the

SOURCE B

'The Government has definitely recognised that there are two distinct elements among the population:- Those who are loyal to the British Crown and Empire, and those who are not. The Government is asking the help of all loyalists in Ulster and proposes to arm with firearms all those called on for duty, to confer certain privileges, to recognise them and to indemnify them for injuries incurred by the performance of their duties.'

Memo from Lt. Col. W. Spender to all officers commanding the Belfast battalions of the UVF, 29 Oct 1920.

SOURCE C

A group of B Specials pose beside an armoured car in the early 1920s.

Catholic population in the North. Violence increased as 1921 wore on, and in one particularly savage week in November, 27 people were killed in Belfast. Over 100 had died from violence in the city that year. With the IRA campaign over in the South, Collins was able to devote more resources to operations in the North, and a new IRA offensive was launched at the beginning of 1922. In Belfast the violence reached a new peak, and in March a total of 61 people were killed in the city. In a particularly horrific incident one Catholic family had five of its members murdered in their own home. The youngest child had survived by hiding under a table. A few weeks later a Unionist MP was shot dead in a Belfast street on his way to work. There was also a series of IRA attacks along the border of Northern Ireland, which had just been established, and for a few days the IRA actually occupied a small area of territory close to Belleek in County Fermanagh.

In the final six months of The Troubles up to the end of May 1922 nearly 250 people had been killed, nearly all of them civilians. Twice as many Catholics were killed as Protestants, and the Catholic population in the North felt itself cut off from their fellow countrymen in the rest of the country, without protection and at the mercy of the Specials. Although Collins was deeply disturbed by their plight, he had more immediate problems, as both Sinn Fein and the IRA split apart following the signing of a treaty with the British at the end of 1921. In the first three months of 1922 Collins had met Craig on two occasions in London, as efforts were made to halt the killings in the North, but these attempts were unsuccessful. In fact, The Troubles only ended with the outbreak of civil war in the South at the end of June 1922, as the divisions within Sinn Fein reached crisis point.

SOURCE D

"The Unionists were running down the street apparently with a view of engaging the two boys and the Sinn Feiners at the other end and a ... row there would have been but I got in front of our lot and ordered them back..."

SOURCE E

"When [we] were going out to church Robert Johnston and another man came in at the gate and reported that they had got notices to leave the district and that several houses had been attacked and the windows smashed."

SOURCE F

"We have been the only firm who have kept their works open in the district. They have raided several in the vicinity. They threatened to burn down our works because just now we happen to have no RC employees and they want to stop our men and women earning their wages when the RCs can't get into the mills and other places owing to their being closed."

Sources D,E and F all from the diary of F. H. Crawford, July 1920 - April 1923.

?

1 How useful are pictures to an historian studying this period? (**A** and **C**)

2 What can we learn from Source **B** about how Spender expected the UVF to react when the Ulster Special Constabulary was formed?

3 Using Sources **D**, **E** and **F**, explain how The Troubles were affecting Belfast.

4 Sources **D**, **E** and **F** were all written by the Unionist, F H Crawford. How does this affect their reliability?

4.8 Partition

SOURCE A

The Official Opening of the Northern Ireland Parliament, on 21 June 1921, in Belfast City Hall. King George V and Queen Mary are facing the camera.

By the end of the First World War it had become clear that political leaders at Westminster wanted the Irish question removed from British politics. Even the Conservatives had grown tired of the issue, and the once unshakeable bond between them and the Ulster Unionists was no longer as strong. On the other side, the IPP had been wiped out by Sinn Fein, while the Liberal party was deeply divided and destined for the political wilderness. Although Lloyd George remained Prime Minister following the 1918 general election, he was head of a coalition government dominated by the Conservatives. The Coalition (which meant that different parties joined together in government) had been formed in 1915 to boost Britain's war effort, and it was decided to continue with this form of government in the immediate postwar period.

THE GOVERNMENT OF IRELAND ACT 1920

While both The Troubles and the Anglo-Irish War had been in progress, Lloyd George had directed a cabinet committee under the chairmanship of the old Southern Unionist, **Walter Long**, to come up with a new political settlement for Ireland. The guideline followed by the committee was that any solution should be on the basis of a fourth Home Rule Bill, but this time special provision would be made for Ulster. The new measure, which was known as the **Government of Ireland Bill**, was introduced in the House of Commons in February 1920. Its main proposal was **partition**. The government wanted to establish two new parliaments in Ireland, one for the six counties of North-East Ulster, and the other for

SOURCE B

"Mr Asquith dealt in greater detail last night with the Irish problem. His solution is still complete self-determination for the whole of Ireland. He paid a tribute to Ulster as the mainspring of Ireland's prosperity, and professed disbelief in that prosperity suffering under Nationalist rule. He for his part would risk the prospect of the majority in Ireland proclaiming an independent Republic, but made no statement as to how Ulster's prosperity was to be insured against that risk."

Belfast News-Letter, 3 February 1920. Mr. Asquith's speech was made in Paisley, Scotland.

SOURCE C

"Major L. Moore, Unionist candidate for East Donegal ... said the Roman Catholics of Derry and elsewhere in the North of ireland were out for a 'whole Ulster', their reason being that they hoped by peaceful penetration with which they had already succeeded in Derry to gain a majority in Ulster."

Belfast News-Letter, 27 February 1920.

SOURCE D

"Ulster is to be given a month to decide as to her future status. Should she stand by the Act of 1920 a Boundary Commission will be set up ' to determine the boundaries between Northern Ireland and the rest of Ireland.'"

Belfast News-Letter, 7 December 1921.

the remaining twenty-six counties. As was the case with Home Rule, both of these new parliaments were to have very limited powers.

It was only at the last moment that the government decided to exclude six rather that the nine counties of Ulster. In reaching this decision cabinet ministers had bowed to pressure from Ulster Unionist leaders who knew that they would enjoy a safe majority in a six county parliament, whereas their position in a nine county parliament would have been precarious. The three counties left out, **Cavan, Monaghan** and **Donegal** all had substantial Nationalist majorities. Naturally, there was a howl of protest from Unionists living in these three counties, who felt that they had been betrayed in these final negotiations by the Unionist leadership, but in March 1920 the Ulster Unionist Council decided to accept the offer of a six county parliament. When the Government of Ireland Act was passed in December 1920, a newly partitioned state, Northern Ireland, was created.

THE 1921 ELECTIONS

Elections for the two parliaments were due in May 1921. Unionists, to their surprise, won 40 of the 52 seats in the new **Northern Ireland Parliament**, giving them the comfortable majority which they had expected. The other 12 seats were shared equally between the IPP and Sinn Fein, who had made an electoral deal before voting took place. The new parliament, which sat in Belfast City Hall, was opened by the King in **June 1921**, and while it was a great propaganda success, the new state was soon facing a struggle for its very existence, as violence increased in the autumn of that year.

The elections for the **Southern Ireland Parliament** were a farce. Nationalist opinion had clearly moved far beyond any Home Rule type offer of a settlement, with Sinn Fein demanding an independent republic, and the Anglo-Irish War raging in the South. Not surprisingly, therefore, the Government of Ireland Act, as it applied to the South, was totally ignored by Sinn Fein. The party simply used the opportunity of an election to return 124 Sinn Feiners unopposed for a new Dail which again declared its allegiance to an Irish Republic. Four Unionists were also elected for Dublin University.

THE TREATY DECEMBER 1921

A political settlement with the South only arrived in December 1921, when the **Anglo-Irish Treaty** was signed, granting much more freedom to the South than had been proposed under the terms of the Government of Ireland Act. As far as the Lloyd George government was concerned, the Irish question was no longer a factor in British politics.

SOURCE E

'Northern Ireland is to have power within a month to enter the Free State or to remain outside it and retain its present position.'

The Irish Times, 7 December 1921.

1   With which parts of Asquith's speech would Unionists (a) agree, (b) disagree? (**B**)

2   Explain why the view taken in Source **C** would be supported by Unionists?

3   The Government of Ireland Act (Source **F**) specifically outlined a six county Northern Ireland. How do Sources **D** and **E** indicate that such a position was not permanent?

4   Explain how Southern Unionists would have reacted to the partition of Ireland.

SOURCE F

'The Bill proposes to establish separate Parliaments for Southern and Northern Ireland. Northern Ireland is to consist of the Parliamentary Counties of Antrim, Armagh, Down, Derry, Fermanagh and Tyrone, and the Parliamentary Boroughs of Belfast and Derry ...

...A Council ... is to be constituted ... The Council will be composed of a President, appointed by the King, and forty members chosen equally by the two Houses of Commons ...

There is a prohibition against laws interfering with Religious equality ...

The two Houses of Commons are to consist of:- Southern Ireland, 128 members; Northern Ireland, 52 members.

The principle of proportional representation is to apply to the elections ...

There are to be 42 Irish members in the House of Commons of the United Kingdom ...

The Bill proposes to repeal the Home Rule Act of 1914.'

The Irish Times, 28 February 1920.

4.9 The Geography of Partition

The negotiations leading up to the Anglo-Irish Treaty saw both sides make compromises. Sinn Fein was not granted the independent republic which it had demanded, but the twenty-six counties, now known as the **Irish Free State**, did receive almost total freedom from British rule. Despite their protests, the Irish representatives were unable to do anything about partition, but they did receive a promise from the British that a **Boundary Commission** would be appointed to suggest changes to the new border running between Northern Ireland and the Irish Free State. This caused great anxiety for the Unionist leaders, because it was likely that such a commission would recommend the transfer of territory along the border, where there was a Nationalist majority, to the Irish Free State. Parts of **South Down**, **South Armagh**, in addition to large areas of **Tyrone** and **Fermanagh**, could be handed over to the Irish Free State in any such arrangement. After all the boundary was really only an artificial dividing line which took no account of geographic or economic factors.

The treaty negotiations at the end of 1921 revealed the British attitude to partition. They disliked it and did not think it would last. An earlier indication of the British view of partition as a temporary measure appeared in the Government of Ireland Act itself, because the measure made provision for the establishment of a **Council of Ireland**. This body was to include representatives from both the Dublin and Belfast parliaments, and its brief was to deal with matters of common concern. The aim behind the Council of Ireland was to smooth the path to eventual unity which even Conservative party leaders considered inevitable.

SOURCE A

"It was represented that a Parliament for the nine Counties would have a Nationalist and Sinn Fein majority ... The population of Ulster was:-

Protestants	890,880
Roman Catholics	690,816
Leaving a Protestant	
majority of	200,064

...The new Bill gives Ulster 64 members and that if there had been 64 in the last election the numbers would have been:-

Unionists	38
Nationalists	26

Giving a Unionist majority of 12

...There are more Unionists in the Southern [ie Irish Free State] area than there are Nationalists in the three counties and no provision whatever is made for them."

From *Ulster and Home Rule: No Partition of Ulster*. Statement by the delegates for Cavan, Donegal and Monaghan, 1921.

SOURCE B

Saint Patrick's Day card, issued about 1922, showing the new Northern Ireland border.

SOURCE C

Sir James Craig, the first Prime Minister of Northern Ireland, (1921-40).

SOURCE D

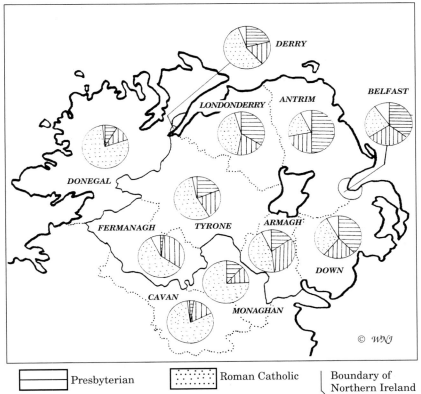

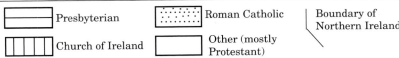

The partition of Ulster showing the border of Northern Ireland and the boundaries of the nine Ulster counties. The pie graphs show the religious breakdown of each county in the census of 1911.

Partition, of course, was a compromise. Ever since 1913 it had presented itself as a solution which might accommodate both Unionists and Nationalists. Redmond had been opposed to any measure which would not treat Ireland as one nation, but by March 1914 he had reluctantly accepted the principle of partition as the price of peace. What made partition almost inevitable was the government's repeated refusal to coerce the Ulster Unionists into accepting any settlement on an all-Ireland basis.

Yet partition had obvious limitations. It created two new states which were mutually hostile, and this hostility was to continue for many years. Moreover, partition had left Northern Ireland with a substantial Catholic minority - about a third of the total population. From the outset, much of this minority remained Nationalist and opposed the very existence of the new state, and it has continued to demand the removal of the border and the reunification of Ireland.

SOURCE E

"It is reported that the leaders of the Sinn Fein factions have come to a secret agreement, the result of which will be that 'Dail Eireann' will express approval of the 'Treaty'.
In the meantime the campaign to bring pressure on the Republicans is in full blast, and the latest voice to join the chorus is that of Mr. Lloyd George himself, who, in a manifesto from Cannes, says that even the alteration of the 'Treaty' would render it null and void.
Mr. Lloyd George holds out three lures to induce the opponents of the agreement to accept it - (1) Evacuation of Southern Ireland by British troops, (2) The release of the Sinn Fein convicts, (3) The immediate handing over to a 'Provisional Government' of Executive Authority."

Belfast News-Letter, 29 December 1921.

1. What arguments were put forward by the Unionists of Donegal, Cavan and Monaghan against their exclusion from Northern Ireland? (A)

2. Why do you think Source B was issued and how was it to be used?

3. Using the information in Source D and the rest of this section, explain why the Unionists were prepared to accept partition of the six counties.

4. What would have been the likely effect of Lloyd George's statement on the Irish Nationalists? (E)

HENRY HERBERT ASQUITH 1852 - 1928.

Liberal politician; supported Gladstone on the Home Rule issue. Home Secretary 1892 - 1894, Chancellor of the Exchequer 1905 - 1908. Prime Minister 1908 - 1916. Introduced Third Home Rule Bill 1912. Prime Minister during the Curragh Incident in March 1914 and the Buckingham Palace Conference in July 1914. In May 1916 he visited Dublin to prevent further executions. In December 1916 Lloyd-George replaced him as Prime Minister.

ARTHUR BALFOUR 1848 - 1930.

Conservative politician. Chief Secretary in Ireland 1887 - 1891, during which much coercion was used. This gained him the nickname of 'Bloody Balfour'. He did however have a somewhat enlightened approach to the land question. Opposed to Home Rule. Replaced as leader of the Conservatives by Andrew Bonar-Law in 1911.

ANDREW BONAR-LAW 1858 - 1923.

A Scots Canadian with Ulster family connections. Gave his full support to the Ulster Unionist resistance to Home Rule. Joined Carson at the Balmoral demonstration against the Third Home Rule Bill in 1912. In July of that year he spoke at a mass meeting at Blenheim Palace, saying that he could understand the Ulsterman's resistance and their need to use force if necessary.

ISAAC BUTT 1813 - 1879.

Son of a Church of Ireland rector in Donegal. Became a barrister and later Professor of Political Economy at Trinity College, Dublin. In his twenties he was a Unionist but his political views changed as a result of the Famine and his defence of the Young Irelanders. This gave him the idea of a Federal solution for Ireland. Later his defence of the Fenians led him to demand self-government. He formed the Home Government Association in 1873. Lost the leadership to Parnell.

EDWARD CARSON 1854 - 1935.

A Dublin barrister who also practised law in London. MP for Trinity College, Dublin from 1890. He became leader of the Unionists in 1910. Took a leading role in the formation of the UVF in 1912. He was Attorney-General in 1915 but resigned because he disagreed over the conduct of the war. Took office as First Lord of the Admiralty in 1916 when Lloyd-George assured him of the exclusion of the six counties. After the war he became MP for Duncairn, Belfast. Life peerage in 1921. When he died in 1935 he was given a state funeral. Buried in St. Anne's Cathedral, Belfast.

MICHAEL COLLINS 1890 - 1922.

Born in Clonakilty, Co. Cork. Went to London in 1906 and worked as a clerk. Joined the Gaelic Athletic Association. He returned briefly to Ireland in 1915 when he joined the IRB. There he met Plunkett, MacDermott and Clarke. In 1916 he was aide-de-camp to Plunkett in the General Post Office during the Easter Rising. Member of the Provisional Executive of the Irish Volunteers. Minister of Home Affairs and Finance in the first Dail. Signed the Treaty of December 1921, and led the pro-Treaty section during the Civil War. Killed in an ambush in 1922.

JAMES CONNOLLY 1869 - 1916.

Born Co. Monaghan. Family emigrated to Edinburgh. Returned to Ireland and then on to America for three years. Returned to Ireland to organise the Labour movement. Helped form the Irish Citizen Army which joined the Irish Volunteers in Easter Rising 1916. Commandant General of Dublin Division of Irish Citizen Army during the Rising. Executed May 1916 in Kilmainham Jail.

JAMES CRAIG 1871 - 1940.

Son of a distillery millionaire. Worked as a stock-broker and had his own firm. Became a Captain in the Royal Irish Rifles during the Boer War. MP for East Down 1906 - 1918. Prominent Unionist, second to Carson. Knighted 1918. Created "Viscount Craigavon" 1927. After the war he became MP for mid-Down. Became first Prime Minister of Northern Ireland 1921 until death.

MICHAEL DAVITT 1846 - 1906.

Family moved to Lancashire in 1850 following eviction from their Co. Mayo home. Joined the Irish Republican Brotherhood and was involved in the raid on Chester Castle. Was Chief arms purchaser for the Fenians until 1870 when he was imprisoned for fifteen years. Released in 1877 to go to USA. There met John Devoy and returned to Co. Mayo in 1879 to lead land agitation. Formed the Land League, involving Parnell in the New Departure.

EAMONN DE VALERA 1882 - 1975.

Born in New York. Father was Spanish-American. Lived in New York for two years and then went to Ireland to live with his mother's family in Co. Limerick.

5.1

Became a mathematics teacher, a member of the Gaelic League and a founder member of the Irish Volunteers in 1913. Commanded the rebels in Boland's Mill during the Rising. Due for execution but stopped by Asquith. Probably saved because of his American birth. Imprisoned, released 1917 and became leader of the new Sinn Fein and of the Volunteers. Arrested and imprisoned again in 1918. Elected first President of the Dail. Led the anti-Treaty group in the Civil War. Formed his own party, Fianna Fail, in 1926.

JOHN DILLON 1851 - 1921.
Educated in Dublin at Royal College of Surgeons. Leading agitator in the Land League. Advocated the boycotting action. Went to USA with Parnell in 1879 where they raised £30,000 for the cause. Leader in the Plan of Campaign. Imprisoned 1887 under coercion. After Redmond's death in 1918 he became leader of the Irish Parliamentary Party.

WILLIAM EWART GLADSTONE 1809 - 1898.
Liberal politician. Prime Minister 1864 - 1874. Disestablished the Church in Ireland in 1869 and passed the Land Act in 1870. Second term as Prime Minister 1880 - 1886 during which there was Land League agitation. Signed the Kilmainham Treaty with Parnell in 1882. Introduced the First Home Rule Bill in 1886. Third term as PM 1892 - 1894 during which he introduced the Second Home Rule Bill.

ARTHUR GRIFFITH 1871 - 1922.
Dublin journalist. Founded a small political party called Sinn Fein, 1905. He wanted Ireland to be a separate independent country, although he was originally prepared to accept Edward VII as King in name only. Imprisoned 1916. Released December of the same year. Was with Collins in London when the Treaty was negotiated in December 1921. Suffered a stroke and died in 1922 during the Civil War.

DAVID LLOYD-GEORGE 1863 - 1945.
British Liberal. Prime Minister 1916 - 1922. In May 1917 he proposed excluding the six north-eastern counties from Home Rule. Refused to recognise Dail Eireann when it was set up in December 1918. Introduced the Government of Ireland Act, 1920. Was responsible for sending the 'Black and Tans' and Auxiliaries to Ireland during the Troubles. He negotiated the Treaty of December 1921.

EOIN MACNEILL 1867 - 1945.
Born Glenarm, Co. Antrim. Educated St. Malachy's College, Belfast. Studied Irish at University College, Dublin. Became founder vice-president of the Gaelic League. Later he became the League's President. Took the lead in the formation of the Irish Volunteers, November 1913. Editor of IVF official paper *Irish Volunteer*. Cancelled Volunteer activity for Easter 1916 when he heard of the plans for the Rising. Arrested early in Easter Week and sentenced to penal servitude but later released.

CHARLES STEWART PARNELL 1846 - 1891.
Protestant landowner who became leader of Home Rule Party. Also was President of the Land League, so linking the land question to the Home Rule issue. Became MP for Co. Meath 1875. Exercised the policy of obstruction in Westminster. Imprisoned in Kilmainham Jail in 1881. Released after six months on condition that he would use his influence to restore order in the country. In 1890 his long-standing affair with Kitty O'Shea became public when her husband sought a divorce. This brought condemnation from the Roman Catholic Church and ended his political career. He died the next year.

PATRICK PEARSE 1879 - 1916.
Educated by Christian Brothers. A barrister who spoke both Irish and English. Wrote poetry, prose and plays in both languages. Founded the Scoil Éanna (a bilingual school) for boys. A member of the Military Council of the Irish Republican Brotherhood. Commander-in-Chief of Provisional Government. Executed for his part in the Easter Rising, in Kilmainham Jail, May 1916.

JOHN REDMOND 1856 - 1918.
MP for New Ross 1881 - 1885. An able speaker. Toured Australia and USA during 1883 - 1884. Lawyer. Called to the English Bar 1885, and the Irish Bar 1887. Supported Parnell during the split in the Home Rule Party in 1890. Became leader of the remnant of the party after the split. Remained the prominent Home Rule leader during the period. Encouraged Irish Volunteers to join the British Army in 1914 in the hope of gaining Home Rule as a reward.

75

5.2 General Elections and Prime Ministers

	Nov 1868	Feb 1874	Apr 1880	Nov 1885
Conservatives and Unionists	279	352	238	251
Liberals	379	243	352	333
Irish Nationalists	-	59	62	86*

Irish Nationalists in these tables mean supporters of Home Rule. In Parliament this group was referred to as the **Irish Parliamentary Party (IPP)**. However, Irish Nationalists include **Independent Nationalists** who were not in the IPP.

	Jul 1886	Jul 1892	Jul 1895	Feb 1900
Conservatives and Unionists	316	269	340	334
Liberal Unionists	78	46	71	68
Liberals	191	273	177	186
Irish Nationalists	85*	81*	82*	82*

The figures are for the **whole** of the UK. Until 1885 there were 658 seats (of which 103 were for Ireland). After 1885 there were 670 seats (Ireland 103).

Throughout these tables the figure for **Conservatives** includes Unionists elected for **Irish** constituencies.

	Jan 1906	Jan 1910	Dec 1910
Conservatives and Unionists	156	273	272
Liberals	379	275	272
Irish Nationalists	83*	82*	84*
Labour and Trade Union	52	40	42

*One elected for an English constituency

In 1886 the Liberal Party split over the Home Rule issue. Those Liberals who opposed Home Rule were known as the **Liberal Unionists** and allied themselves with the Conservatives.

After 1900 the Liberal Unionists were regarded as part of the Conservative Party. The figure for **Labour** in 1906 includes 24 MPs who supported the Liberals and were known as **Lib-Lab**.

Government Coalition Parties	Dec 1918 Election		Opposition Parties
Conservatives and Unionists	383	63	Labour
Liberals	133	28	Asquith Liberals
Coalition Labour	10	7*	Irish Nationalists
		73	Sinn Fein

*Six elected for Irish seats and one in England.

The 1918 election was unique. During the War there had been a **Coalition Government** (Conservative, Liberal, Labour) led first by Asquith and then Lloyd George. It was decided to continue this Coalition until a peace settlement had been drawn up, but most of the Labour Party and some of the Liberals would not co-operate. In Ireland the Irish Nationalists had been decimated by the rise of **Sinn Fein**. The Sinn Fein MPs refused to attend Parliament and in January 1919 set up the **Dail** in Dublin.

BRITISH PRIME MINISTERS 1868 - 1922

Prime Minister	Government	Dates
W.E. Gladstone	Liberal	Dec1868 - Feb1874
Benjamin Disraeli	Conservative	Feb1874 - Apr1880
W.E. Gladstone	Liberal	Apr1880 - Jun1885
Lord Salisbury	Conservative	Jun1885 - Jan1886
W.E. Gladstone	Liberal	Jan1886 - July1886
Lord Salisbury	Conservative	July1886 - Aug1892
W.E. Gladstone	Liberal	Aug1892 - Mar1894
Lord Rosebery	Liberal	Mar1894 - Jun1895
Lord Salisbury	Conservative	Jun1895 - July1902
A.J. Balfour	Conservative	July1902 - Dec1905
Henry Campbell-Bannerman	Liberal	Dec1905 - Apr1908
Herbert Asquith	Liberal	Apr1908 - May1915
Herbert Asquith	Coalition	May1916 - Dec1916
David Lloyd George	Coalition	Dec1916 - Oct1922

5.3 Chronology

1858	-Formation of the **Irish Republican Brotherhood** (IRB), or Fenian Movement.
1867	-Fenian Rising.
1869	-Church of Ireland Disestablished.
1870	-Gladstone's First Land Act.
	-**Home Rule Association** formed by Isaac Butt.
1875	-Parnell elected MP.
1879	-**Land League** formed.
1880	-Parnell elected Chairman of the Irish Parliamentary Party(IPP).
	-Boycotting Campaign begins.
1881	-Gladstone's Second Land Act.
	-Parnell imprisoned.
1882	-Kilmainham 'Treaty'.
	-Phoenix Park murders.
1884	-Formation of the **Gaelic Athletic Association (GAA)**.
1885	-Irish Loyal and Patriotic Union formed.
1886	-Ulster Loyalist Anti-Repeal Union formed.
	-**First Home Rule Bill**.
	-'Plan of Campaign' begins.
1887	-Piggott forgeries published in The Times.
1890	-O'Shea divorce case.
	-Irish Parliamentary Party splits over Parnell.
1891	-Death of Parnell; John Redmond leads the Parnellites.
	-Irish Loyal and Patriotic Union replaced by the **Irish Unionist Alliance**.
1893	-**Second Home Rule Bill**.
	-Formation of the **Gaelic League**.
1900	-Irish Parliamentary Party (Home Rule Party) reunited under Redmond.
1905	-Ulster Unionist Council formed.
	-**Sinn Fein** movement founded.
1908	-Asquith becomes Prime Minister.
1910	-Carson becomes leader of the Irish Unionists.
1911	-**Parliament Act** restricts the power of the House of Lords.
	-Unionist Demonstrations.
1912	-**Third Home Rule Bill** introduced (April).
	-**Solemn League and Covenant** (28 Sept).
1913	-**Ulster Volunteer Force** (UVF) formed (Jan).
	-Provisional Government set up in Ulster (Sept).
	-**Irish Volunteer Force** set up (Nov).
	-**Irish Citizen Army** formed (Nov).
1914	-Curragh incident (Mar).
	-**Larne Gun-Running** by UVF (April).
	-Buckingham Palace Conference (July).
	-**Howth Gun-Running** by IVF (July).
	-Outbreak of the First World War (Aug).
	-Third Home Rule Bill becomes law. (Sept).
	-Recruitment issue splits the Irish Volunteers (Sept).
1916	-**Easter Rising** (April).
	-Battle of the Somme begins (July).
1917	-'New' Sinn Fein movement emerges.
	-Hunger Strikes.
	-**Irish Convention**.
1918	-Conscription Crisis.
	-General Election (Dec), Sinn Fein victory in Ireland.
1919	-**Dail Eireann** meets (Jan).
	-Anglo-Irish War begins.
1920	-**Black and Tans** formed.
	-Sectarian strife in Ulster.
	-Ulster Special Constabulary (**B-Specials**) formed (Sept).
	-'Bloody Sunday' (Nov).
	-**Government of Ireland Act** passed (Dec).
1921	-Elections for the two Irish parliaments.
	-Northern Ireland set up (June).
	-**Truce** in the South between the IRA and the British (July).
	-**Treaty** between Sinn Fein and the British (Dec).

Glossary

Act	The name given to a new law that has been passed.
Amendment	Changes to a Bill before it becomes law.
Bill	The name given to a law that is still being discussed.
Boycott	To shun another or treat him as an outcast.
By-election	Election held when an MP has died or resigned.
Coalition	Different parties joined together in a government.
Coercion	Use of force.
Conscription	Being called to do compulsory military service.
Emancipation	Freeing. In Ireland this meant the end of restrictions placed on Roman Catholics.
Eviction	Removing a tenant by force from his house or farm.
Home Rule	Desire to have one's own parliament for home affairs.
Imperial	Belonging to an Empire.
Industrial Revolution	Change from cottage system of industry to factories from mid18th century.
Landlord	A man who owns property and lets it for rent.
Nationalism	Movement to set up an independent nation-state.
Obstruction	A tactic used by Irish MPs to delay debates in Parliament and make their cause heard.
Partition	A division. In Ireland used to mean the division of the island into two parts in 1921.
Provisional Government	A government which would rule the country until a permanent one is elected.
Sectarian	Concerned with different religions or sects.
Segregation	Keeping different groups apart.
Tenant farmer	A farmer who rents property from another, known as his landlord.
Unionism	Oppostition to Home Rule; support for the union with Britain.

Index